Contents

...he most successful young

...blishing Ltd,
...N9 2ND

...ate Walters

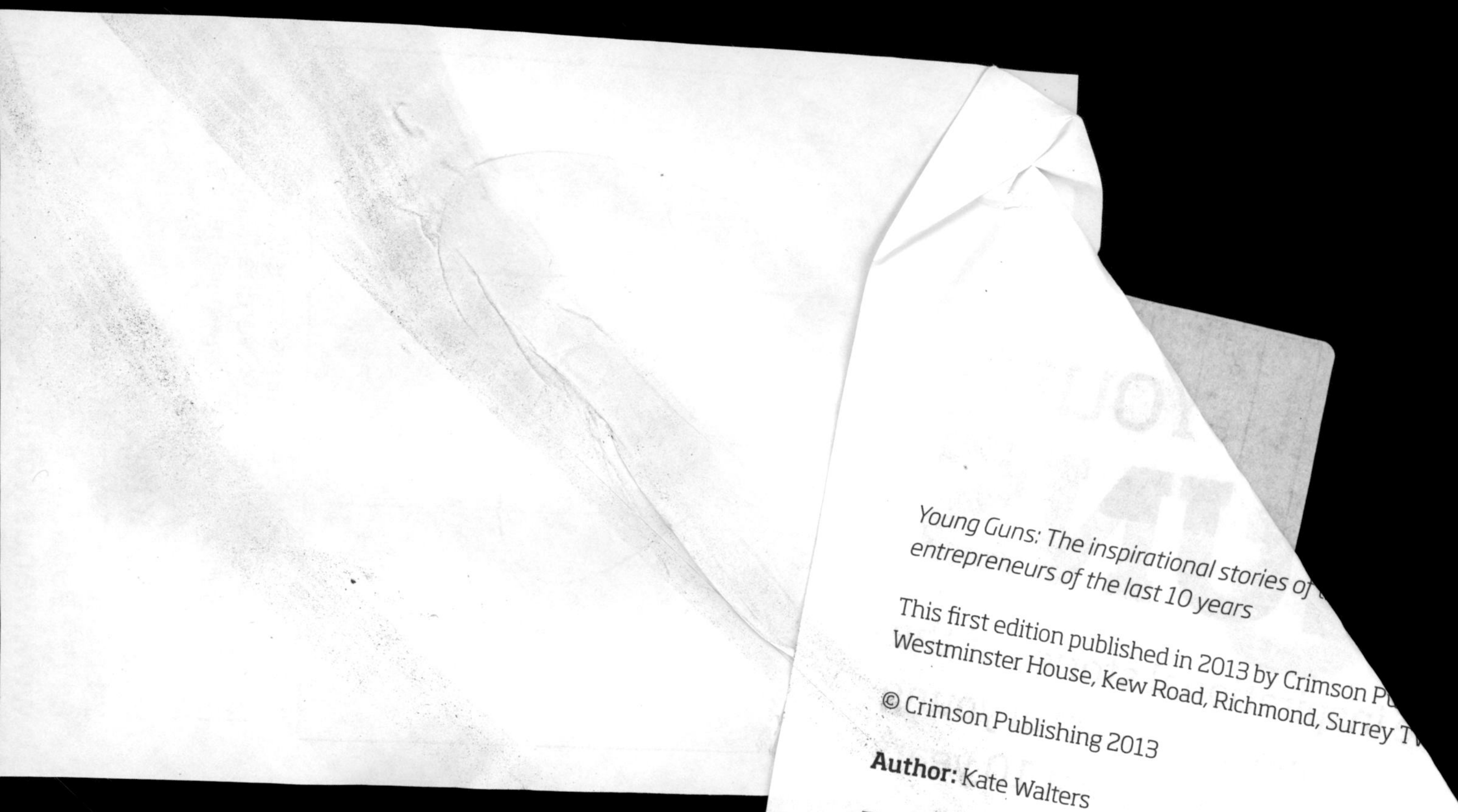

Young Guns: The inspirational stories of
entrepreneurs of the last 10 years

This first edition published in 2013 by Crimson Pu
Westminster House, Kew Road, Richmond, Surrey T

Author: Kate Walters

Th

Foreword

By Michael Acton Smith, founder and CEO of Mind Candy

Ten years ago and long before I dreamt up Moshi Monsters, I was named a Young Gun by *Growing Business* magazine. This new list did something you didn't see that often in the UK back then. It celebrated the early success and potential of Britain's next generation of young entrepreneurs.

I gather the inspiration came from *Vanity Fair* magazine, which dedicated a cover each year to Hollywood's rising stars, photographed by the iconic Annie Leibovitz. Each 'class' featured the future of the film industry. Young Guns sought to do the same for British business, reflecting the energy and excitement of entrepreneurship.

My company, Firebox, which I'd started with Tom Boardman, had a venture capital backer and a few million pounds of revenue. I was excited but nervous when selected as a Young Gun and didn't quite know what to expect when I rocked up at a small photographer's studio in Islington, London.

Growing Business had done a very impressive job of picking future winners. Among that inaugural group were the founders of Agent Provocateur, Nails Inc, Innocent Drinks, Cardpoint, Myla, Currencies Direct and Printing.com. We posed for photos and got to know each other over a few drinks. I'm happy to say that I'm still friends with a few of the group, a decade on from that first meeting. A more recent Young Guns event started serenely over lunch at Kensington Roof Gardens but ended up in a Soho dive bar at 3 a.m. the next morning, but that's a story best left for another day.

The bonds and friendships forged in the heat of building entrepreneurial businesses can often last a lifetime. This is why Young Guns, for me, stands for more than a seal of approval and recognition. It symbolises what is great about entrepreneurship and why your peers in business are so much a part of what you do.

Moshi Monsters may now have 80 million users spread over 150 countries, but back then it wasn't even a seedling of an idea and might never have sparked into life were it not for having a network of friends, investors and advisers.

It's part of why I now host Silicon Drinkabout in the heart of London's tech city every Friday to bring start-ups together, and it's why I try to attend as many events and conferences around the world as I can.

Young Guns brought me closer to some of the UK's most outstanding entrepreneurs from a variety of different sectors. It provided a great networking opportunity each year to meet the next 'class' destined for big things.

The life of an entrepreneur isn't easy. It's a roller-coaster ride of highs and lows, late nights, red-eye flights and obstacles. There are obviously many amazing moments on the journey but you definitely need a strong resolve to cope with the setbacks. Given the challenges involved, it's vital you pick an area that you are passionate about to help weather the storm.

When Tom and I decided to leave our sensible jobs and set up in business, we didn't really know what area to focus on. We really wanted to be entrepreneurs and knew we were going to be spending countless hours devoted to it so it had to be something fun that we were really interested in.

We used to have sensible conversations in the local pub discussing business ideas. Gadgets and games took up much of the conversation so that seemed like a smart place to dive into. Work and play merged and life became one intense but fascinating adventure.

Find a job you love and you never have to work another day in your life – it's great advice.

We didn't have enough cash to start a catalogue or a shop so we felt the internet would be the best area to focus on. This was back in 1998 and life as a technology entrepreneur wasn't easy. There weren't many competitors but there weren't many customers either. Most people looked at us blankly when we told them we were launching an online shop.

So much has changed since those early days. The internet has gone mainstream and there are now over 2 billion people online around the world. That creates extraordinary opportunities for nimble and creative entrepreneurs to launch exciting new businesses. Nimble start-ups that can adapt rapidly to new technologies, devices and platforms have a big advantage over the slower-moving corporations. In fact, this is one of the best times in history to be an entrepreneur.

Enjoy the book, be inspired and dream big!

Introduction: The Young Guns awards

Talk to someone long enough and you're likely to find, hidden away, their idea for a new business. So many of us secretly dream of going it alone, bringing an idea to life in the ultimate rejection of the 9 to 5. But this book is about the people who didn't merely dream, sketching out their business ideas on napkins in idle moments only to do nothing about it. This book is about the people who took a risk and decided that there was a gap in the market that they themselves could fill. And every single one of them did this while still in their twenties, early thirties, or even teens. Optimists, dreamers, overachievers: it is these people the Young Guns awards were founded to celebrate.

Back in the early 2000s, entrepreneurship was yet to become sexy. Wildly successful business programmes on prime time TV did not exist. This was before the new breed of Silicon Valley tech geeks struck gold with Facebooks and Twitters, and in doing so opened people's minds to the possibility of entrepreneurship as a young person's game. Young Guns was formed in 2003 by *Growing Business* magazine, which was mindful of the need to give the UK's entrepreneurs - particularly the precocious young people starting to make waves in almost every sector - the recognition they deserved but rarely received.

The inaugural Young Guns award ceremony wasn't the swish, champagne-fuelled extravaganza that it would become over the years. But this low-key event marked the first of a decade - and counting - of the annual event, at which selected entrepreneurs, all aged 35 or under, behind 30 of the UK's most promising, innovative, fast-growth businesses gather for an afternoon of networking and celebration.

The individuals within the remarkable first group of Young Guns set the standard for the level of talent and potential the list would strive to uncover. Gathered together in 2003 were the likes of Richard Reed, on the brink of Innocent's rise to dominance over the soft-drinks sector; Michael Acton Smith, who went on to create children's entertainment phenomenon Moshi Monsters; Mayank Patel, who has since received an OBE for services to British business and whose firm, Currencies Direct, turns over something in the region of £2 billion a year; as well as the founders of businesses such as Agent Provocateur, Nails Inc and Gamestation.

Since that first year, the Young Guns list has built a track record for unearthing phenomenal business talent. Hundreds of entrepreneurs have been identified on their ascent to greatness. But, as is only to be expected, some of the individuals in the following pages haven't always met with success. What no one knew in 2003 was how tough things were going to get. As the credit crunch started to bite, accessing start-up capital became increasingly difficult. Entrepreneurs were required to be ever more creative and industrious in order to find ways of thriving. Even if businesses, particularly those in sectors where costs of entry can be high, could find enough funding to bring an idea to market, it became harder to justify taking the big risks and dreaming the big dreams that are often needed for something special to be created.

As consumers' purse strings tightened, so did the margins of many thousands of firms - from start-ups through to FTSE 100s. Larger businesses (though by no means all of them) were sometimes able to swallow the losses. For smaller firms, it could be much more difficult. Retail businesses in particular have had to cope with a prolonged period of cost inflation. This has left them in the unenviable position of having to choose between passing on the rising costs or sacrificing margins. For a company just beginning to grab some market share and gain some brand recognition, a hefty dose of luck, as well as sound financial, commercial and marketing sense, is often needed to ensure that this doesn't spell failure.

So it's no surprise that among the 300 or so businesses in the following pages, there are some that didn't make it through what has been the worst economic crisis in living memory. Business people from every sector represented in this book have reluctantly had to close their doors, some in a blaze of publicity. Wedding gift list firm Wrapit was founded by Pepita Diamand, a Young Gun in 2006, and had become Britain's third largest gift list service. However, it wasn't able to ride the turbulent economic waters and its demise in 2009 was much talked and written about. SpinVox, founded by 2006 Young Gun Christina Domecq, was heralded - and not only by the Young Guns judges - as one of the hottest technology start-ups British business had ever seen. But it too crashed to the ground.

It would clearly be disingenuous to claim that the risk of failure isn't an inevitable part of life for most entrepreneurs. Those of a young age can be more susceptible, lacking the experience often needed when the going gets really tough. But one of the things that sets successful entrepreneurs apart is their response to failure. In the US, the phrase 'failing up' is common parlance. To many who have experience of running a business, this is a familiar concept. If one idea doesn't work, learn from it and move on. Many entrepreneurs in this book are no longer with the businesses that brought them to the attention of the Young Guns judges. Some have exited successfully and have set up businesses that have even more potential or are performing even more impressively. Others were forced to close their firms, but have found success with later ventures. Yet others are applying the lessons they've learned through entrepreneurial journeys to angel investing, consulting or inspirational speaking.

But the recession, let's not forget, hasn't exclusively meant doom and gloom. So many businesses have thrived over the last few years. Innumerable entrepreneurs and small businesses have taken advantage of the demise of sector giants. Their nimbleness and their willingness and ability to adapt have meant that smaller firms have often been able to grow even faster than they would have in more temperate times. For firms growing by acquisition, bargains have been plentiful as struggling rivals lie ready for the taking. As the viability of business models has been tested continually, those with firm foundations have more often than not remained strong and able to grow.

The examples of thriving, profitable, well-run businesses in the following chapters overwhelmingly outnumber the ones that didn't quite make it. Many have become high-street names. James Murray Wells was just 22 when his business Glasses Direct was identified by Young Guns judges as being on its way to greatness. Hawk-Eye, which has revolutionised the sporting world with its ball-tracking technology, was only three years old, in its infancy but showing huge promise, when its founder, Paul Hawkins, was named a 2004 Young Gun. Retail successes include Notonthehighstreet.com, Sweaty Betty and my-wardrobe.com – all of them household names. Other firms have built their reputations by shaking up traditional industries or innovating in areas ripe for change: BrewDog, founded by 2009 Young Guns James Watt and Martin Dickie, was built on the premise of brewing classic beers with a contemporary twist. JBW Group, a bailiff firm owned by Jamie Waller, Young Gun of 2010, has focused on bringing transparency and up-to-date technology to the bailiff industry, to great effect. Tony Rafferty, one of the first class of Young Guns, has brought innovation to the conservative printing industry by integrating a crowdsourcing element into Printing.com's revenue model.

Unsurprisingly, an ambitious growth rate that leaves rivals languishing in the dust is something many Young Guns' businesses share. Innocent and Sprue Aegis, both founded by Young Guns, are the only companies ever to appear in *The Sunday Times* Fast Track 100 league for five consecutive years. In 2012, World First, founded by 2007 Young Gun Nick Robinson, made its fourth consecutive appearance, and Global Personals, the brainchild of Young Gun Ross Williams, appeared for the third consecutive time. Monitise has recorded a growth rate of 2,875% since it floated on the Alternative Investment Market (AIM) in 2007, the same year founder Alastair Lukies was named a Young Gun.

There have also been some eye-wateringly lucrative and richly deserved exits. Zef Eisenberg, Young Gun of 2006, sold his business Maximuscle to GlaxoSmithKlein in 2010 for a cool £162m. Ben Hardyment, 2003 Young Gun, saw his DVD rental firm, webflix.co.uk, snapped up by LOVEFiLM (itself co-founded by 2009 Young Gun Graham Bosher) in 2005. Another alumnus of 2003, Stephen Hall's business Gamestation was turning over £35m and had 74 stores by the time it was sold to Blockbuster. Yet another Young Gun of the first year was Serena Rees, whose business Agent Provocateur had become a byword for high-end lingerie by the time it was sold for £60m in 2007. And Fasthosts, the creation of serial entrepreneur and Young Gun of 2005 Andrew Michael, was snapped up for £61.5m in 2005 by German company United Internet, at which point Michael still owned 75% equity and was only 25 years old.

The Young Guns list was created to celebrate these people, and also to thank them. Now more than ever, the efforts of entrepreneurs and those owning and running small businesses are vital for economic recovery, job creation and even Britain's reputation on a global scale. Study after study confirms that the UK's smaller enterprises are proving both resilient and important. One recent report found that Britain needs a further 300,000 entrepreneurs to restore the economy to its pre-recession peak, and that the average small or medium-sized enterprise (SME) was worth £130,000 to the economy. The RSA, which issued the report, noted that the number of large firms has fallen by 11% over the last 10 years, while the number of small firms has risen by 35%.

Whether the government is doing enough to support those running small firms is a matter of debate. Certainly, the banks' unwillingness to lend to smaller enterprises has been noted and there has been no shortage of initiatives to make up the lending shortfall to businesses struggling to raise growth capital or to entrepreneurs looking for start-up funding. The new Business Bank may make an impact in 2013, the Business Growth Fund has been a help to many firms, and tax incentives have been well received. Holly Tucker, co-founder of Notonthehighstreet.com, which was part of the Young Guns list of 2008 says: 'Back then [when Notonthehighstreet.com was founded in 2006], we did feel like there wasn't much support for small businesses either through the government or banks. It is good to see that we're taking steps to support the positive impact small businesses are having on the economy but we still have some way to go.'

In the meantime, awards and recognition such as Young Guns fulfil a valuable role in boosting morale and creating publicity for smaller firms, whose owners often work in a relatively isolated capacity. 'No one ever says well done to the boss,' points out Ross Williams, the entrepreneur behind dating firm Global Personals, and a Young Gun of 2011. 'Entrepreneurs slog their guts out, and they generate a lot of tax. But no one ever gives them any recognition. Awards can be the only way of getting third party validation.'

But a pat on the back is only one benefit of such validation. Suranga Chandratillake, founder of tech success story Blinkx and a Young Gun of 2006, points out that in the early days of smaller companies, feedback is both critically important and hard to come by. For this reason, third party recognition becomes much sought after. 'It's very important externally,' he says. 'Customers, partners, investors – they are all looking for validation, and nothing beats third party award-based recognition.' This, he says, made a huge difference when he took Blinkx to the junior stock market in 2007. 'On what basis could we raise $50m? A big part of that was saying, "Look what these people have said".'

Jamie Waller, who founded bailiff company JBW Group and was named a Young Gun in 2010, emphasises the importance of boosting morale: 'Winning awards is great for the team. Not only do they get a pat on the back internally but they get external recognition (including a party). The key is what awards. JBW are selective in which awards we enter; for example, the National Business Awards, Young Guns and *Sunday Times* Top 100 are recognised.' He advises: 'Never buy awards thinking they will help market a business. This is a good time to recognise that quantity does not beat quality.'

And Holly Tucker points out the impact of PR: 'Winning high-profile awards helps grow our brand awareness and establish Notonthehighstreet.com as a successful, reliable online retailer.

'We're honoured to have been acknowledged by prestigious awards such as Young Guns. Being recognised alongside some of the most established and successful names in the industry is a real testament to everything that we and our sellers work so hard for.'

The diversity shown over 10 years of these awards is clear to see in this book, which profiles every single one of the Young Guns, arranged by sector. Individuals who particularly encapsulate the entrepreneurial spirit on which Young Guns are based, or whose businesses have displayed an astonishingly successful or fascinating trajectory, are profiled in depth. In addition, the first chapter looks at the challenges and opportunities faced by younger entrepreneurs in particular, while the final chapter focuses on what the experiences of the Young Guns can teach all those - young or old - who either have entrepreneurial dreams or have started making their dreams a reality.

What Makes a Young Gun?

It's striking how many well-known, uber-successful entrepreneurs started their businesses at a young age. Richard Branson, Google co-founders Larry Page and Sergey Brin, James Dyson, Alan Sugar, Mark Zuckerberg, Bill Gates: all were launching their own ventures well before they turned 30. Does youth really trump experience when it comes to entrepreneurship? Or do these eminent entrepreneurs have something in them, some quirk of personality or ambition, that makes it almost impossible for them to settle for doing anything else, even at a young age? What's certain is that, while there's no perfect age at which to start a business, there are a few key factors that today's young people have on their side.

The advantages of youth

Firstly, the under-35s have grown up in a world in which a pre-internet age is but a distant memory, if they can remember it at all. Even the very first class of Young Guns, who were brought together a decade ago in 2003, had witnessed and learned from the bursting of the dotcom bubble, and the internet had already fundamentally changed the way people were doing business. We had all started going online more often more productively and much more easily. Since then, the internet has continued to lower barriers to entry when it comes to launching a commercial venture. Often, all it takes to start a business is a computer, an idea and an internet connection. It's not only young people who have taken advantage of this. But they are the ones who have always used the internet for work, and have never had to adapt or be left behind.

When it comes to technology start-ups, in particular, young people have grown up knowing about this complicated and fast-moving sector. Perhaps this is best represented by the dozens of digital start-ups clustered in London's so-called 'Silicon Roundabout' - or 'Tech City' - most of which are run by young, bright and ambitious entrepreneurs. As 27-year-old David Batey, whose business MediaGraph is based in Tech City, says: 'When I was at primary and secondary school the internet was just taking off and then [when I was at] secondary and university, mobile technology was commonplace. The fact that I grew up with this technology and it is second nature to me is a tremendous advantage over people who are even 10 years older. I also believe these massive technological changes have probably made me, and people of my generation, better capable of dealing with cutting-edge and rapid change.'

The fact that I grew up with this technology and it is second nature to me is a tremendous advantage over people who are even 10 years older.

Secondly, a stage-of-life advantage means that young people's circumstances are often much more suited to setting up alone. The statistics tell us that entrepreneurship is inherently a risky business. The prospect of failure looms large over many a start-up. A mortgage and a family to support are factors that can play a huge part in making a regular wage too tempting to sacrifice. As 2011 Young Gun Ross Williams, founder of Global Personals, says: 'The thing about Young Guns is that it shows that when you start young you have less to lose. When you're in your mid-20s, what's the worst that could happen? You have to move back in with your mum and dad? I did that anyway. Later in life, you've got used to a certain level of comfort; you may have a husband or wife or children. But it's easier for young people.' And with the job market not being graduate- or school-leaver-friendly in recent years, many young people haven't had the luxury of choosing between a regular and steady income and trying out their entrepreneurial idea: there are few cushy 9-to-5s tempting bright graduates away from a life of self-employment. Furthermore, as any entrepreneur can testify, setting up your own business can be - and usually is - all-encompassing. The lack of responsibilities or commitments that makes entrepreneurship less risky for many young people also means that they are more likely to be able to give their new enterprise all the time and attention it needs.

In addition, although experience is incredibly valuable, a younger person's relative lack of it needn't be an insurmountable problem. For many successful entrepreneurs, not being entirely familiar with the challenges posed by their sector has meant that they were not put off launching a business in the first place. Instead, young people are more likely to do things differently, and to be more creative in their ideas. Finding a suitable mentor can compensate for the gaps in founders' knowledge, and many of the Young Guns in the following pages have individuals on their boards who have years of experience behind them.

When to ask for help

Certainly, therefore, youth should not stand in the way of bringing a great idea to life. But being a young entrepreneur also has its challenges. One such challenge is the difficulties thrown up by the more administrative elements of running a business. For example, David Batey says: 'We are very strong technically and in our industry but we lack experience in areas such as accounting, law, recruitment, sales, raising finance and customer service, which a more mature business professional may have.' And 23-year-old Ross Harper, co-founder of app developer Wriggle, admits: 'I often find myself responding to an issue with the answer, "I just don't know. I need to speak to someone who has encountered this problem before."' Others may have problems in gaining the trust of potential clients due to their young age. Additionally, but incredibly significantly, older entrepreneurs are more likely to have access to start-up capital.

I often find myself responding to an issue with the answer, 'I just don't know. I need to speak to someone who has encountered this problem before.'

Luckily, however, there is a lot of help available, increasingly so since 2003. Some sources of support and advice might be well hidden, and others somewhat London-centric, but both on- and offline there are a plethora of communities where entrepreneurs can share knowledge of launching and running a start-up. The 28-year-old entrepreneur Travis Lee Street, who has co-founded Applaud Social and ShopOfMe, says that today 'we're seeing an overflowing of entrepreneurial events for youngsters', although he does warn that, in his experience, 'there is still a way to go in bridging the confidence and knowledge gap (e.g. in getting them from excitement to experimentation)'. Mentoring and internship opportunities do exist for young entrepreneurs who seek them out; a willingness to source help and knowledge is crucial for the majority of people starting up.

There are signs that access to start-up capital is also becoming easier. In September 2012, the government launched its Start-Up Loans scheme, which offers loans for entrepreneurs between the ages of 18 and 30. In January 2013, the government put an extra £30m into the scheme, which is chaired by James Caan, meaning it has £110m to lend to new enterprises. Successful businesses typically receive £2,500, which is paid back over five years.

Modern ways of sourcing growth capital are also proving effective. The rise of crowdfunding, for example, is providing an alternative to the traditional friends-and-family round of fundraising. Although crowdfunding originally came to public attention through US sites such as Kickstarter, which mainly raises money for non-profit projects such as bands or artists, there are now a host of websites for businesses looking for funding. These include UK sites - start-ups themselves - Crowdcube (which was established in 2011 and has already funded over 30 pitches with an average £143,500) and Silicon Roundabout-based Seedrs, which has been up and running since 2012.

Other start-ups gain funding from competitions and awards. For example, the Shell LiveWIRE programme offers free online business advice and start-up awards of £1,000 and £10,000 funding to young entrepreneurs in the UK.

Another relatively recent option for entrepreneurs is to apply for a place in an incubator. These for-profit accelerator programmes, of which one of the most famous is LA-based Y Combinator, usually offer funding, mentoring and networking opportunities in exchange for equity. The programmes tend to be highly competitive, but of enormous benefit to successful firms.

Granted, seed capital for young entrepreneurs in the UK is not quite as easily available, or as significant, as in the US's Silicon Valley, for example, where entrepreneurs-turned-angel investors are as common as their pockets are deep. But, although banks might not be lending as much as they did to budding entrepreneurs some years ago, there are still plenty of options for people looking for funding to set up or grow their businesses, and many of those experimenting with more modern methods of raising capital are those under the age of 35.

Furthermore, the more traditional process of pitching for funding has been demystified in recent years by TV shows such as *Dragons' Den*, which has brought the concept of entrepreneurship into people's living rooms on a weekly basis. In fact, among the Young Guns profiled in this book, five of them found their way into the Den: 2010 Young Guns Peter Harrison and Wesley Downham, of FGH Security, received offers from all five Dragons and left with £100,000 from Peter Jones and Theo Paphitis, for example; and 2003 Young Gun Ben Hardyment recently secured the largest individual investment ever made on the show, when Theo Paphitis invested £250,000 in his latest start-up, Zapper.

The new rock and roll

Such media attention has been part of a shift in the public perception of setting up a business, and in the last few years younger people have grown up in a society much more aware - and arguably encouraging - of entrepreneurship as a valid career choice. Part of this shift may be down to turbulent economic conditions. As the trusted facets of an economically stable society have repeatedly failed to provide any security, as banks have been nationalised and large firms have collapsed, the risks inherent in entrepreneurially run ventures have started to shrink in comparison. In fact, more and more people are turning to smaller, fast-growth firms, and the people who run them, as a hugely important source of economic regeneration and growth. Young people with ambitions to create market-leading firms are the ones creating the jobs. It's unsurprising that David Cameron recently told young entrepreneurs of his desire to encourage new businesses, in the hope that Britain can create the next Amazon or Google.

It is for this reason perhaps that entrepreneurialism has been described as the 'new rock and roll', with many business owners gaining a level of celebrity indistinguishable from that of film stars or premiership football players. Arguably, these hard-working, super-smart and creative individuals provide young people with role models deserving of the name. And as 27-year-old David Batey points out, 'celebrity entrepreneurs like Zuckerberg and Dorsey [founder of Twitter] have made [starting a business as a young person] more mainstream', although he adds with a laugh: 'My parents still think I'm dossing around though.'

When one looks at those business figures who have become near legends of entrepreneurship - Branson being perhaps the archetypal successful entrepreneur - certain character traits do seem to present themselves with notable frequency. Certainly, without the confidence to go after available help and funding, entrepreneurs of any age are likely to struggle. Self-belief is something that most successful younger entrepreneurs have in spades. As can be seen in many of the profiles in the following pages, a thick skin is essential armour for the self-employed and ambitious, who will inevitably come up against the word 'no' on a fairly frequent basis. A formidable work ethic is also a prerequisite.

But perhaps there are some character traits that younger people more naturally possess, qualities that can be diluted by years of working for someone else, following orders and repressing instinct. Creativity, persistence, passion, a non-conformist attitude, a desire to challenge the status quo - too often employers aren't able to use young people's talents and personalities to best effect. The fact that the UK is home to masses of exciting businesses, brimming with potential, and run by young people unwilling to park their ideas and work for others instead, is cause for excitement and optimism.

The Young Guns

The award-winning entrepreneurs in each sector

Business services

Daniel Mitchell

Company: The Source
Young Gun in: 2003 (Age: 33)
In 2003, The Source, a company that validates insurance claims for loss or damage to computer equipment, was turning over £16m, and on target for £20m a year. In 2005, Mitchell successfully sold the business for a substantial, undisclosed sum.

Lynn Cosgrave

Company: TrusttheDJ
Young Gun in: 2003 (Age: 33)
Following a stint at the Ministry of Sound, where she started the company's record label, Cosgrave struck out on her own with TrusttheDJ, a talent management agency. Two years on, in 2004, it had raised £2m in venture capital and had become one of the leading global names in its market. Although TTDJ eventually went into administration, Cosgrave remains a director at Safehouse Management, which she founded in 2000.

Robin Powell

Company: Molson Holdings
Young Gun in: 2003 (Age: 34)
Founded in 1996 by Powell and Jonathan Wilson, Bristol-based Molson Holdings hired out construction equipment to some of the biggest construction names as well as for smaller individual needs. In 2003 it employed 58 people and had a turnover of £36m. Since then, the entrepreneurs have formed Molson Group, which is still privately owned by Powell, Wilson and another shareholder, and claims to be the UK's biggest independent dealer in construction equipment.

Chirag Shah

Company: Trading Partners
Young Gun in: 2003 (Age: 32)
By 2003, Shah had made Trading Partners, which provided web-based tools and supply chain optimisation consultancy for its blue-chip clients, a £7m business in less than three years. As chief executive officer (CEO), Shah grew Trading Partners into a multimillion-pound organisation operating in Europe, the USA and China. He left the business in 2011 to start e-sourcing business MarketMaker4, of which he is now chairman. Trading Partners went into administration in 2012.

David Kilpatrick

Company: Edenbrook
Young Gun in: 2003 (Age: 34)
In 1997 Kilpatrick and two colleagues quit their jobs at Oracle to start an independent IT consultancy called Fulcrum. Within two years it had 175 staff and US offices, and it was sold in 2000 to Whittman-Hart. It wasn't long before the trio left to set up another IT consultancy, Edenbrook, with £1m from Elderstreet, the venture capital fund managers. In two years the new company reached a turnover of almost £8m with a workforce of more than 60. The company was included in *The Sunday Times* Tech Track 100 in 2004, 2006, 2007 and 2008, when its customers included Bupa, Royal Bank of Scotland, Lloyds TSB and Whitbread. In 2009, they achieved another successful exit, with Edenbrook being acquired by Hitachi Consulting.

Peter Marson

Company: 4C Associates
Young Gun in: 2003 (Age: 32)
Former management consultant Marson and colleague Ed Ainsworth quit their jobs in 2000 to set up software outsourcing and consultancy firm, 4C Associates, with £900,000 of their own and private individuals' money. By 2003, it had secured FTSE 100 clients including AstraZeneca, Boots and Prudential and was set to make £2m by the end of the year. Today, Marson is non-executive director of the company and is involved as an investor and executive in several other businesses.

Yasmin Halai

Company: Ideal Solutions Systems
Young Gun in: 2003 (Age: 31)
Halai spent seven years as a salesperson before teaming up with brother Shabbir to launch Ideal Solutions Systems in 1999. By 2003, the 42-person company was supplying high-quality, longer-lasting printer cartridges to businesses including insurance firms, solicitors, the travel industry and estate agents. Despite competing with Hewlett Packard, it was on course for a 2004 turnover of £6m. Since then, she has founded companies The Green Desk and YHC Holdings.

Mark Mills

Company: Cardpoint
Young Gun in: 2003 (Age: 33)
Mills moves at a frightening pace. A year before he was named a Young Gun in 2003, his company, ATM operator Cardpoint, had just listed on AIM and had 300 machines. Within a year, it had bought two competitors, one a subsidiary of Securicor, for £9.2m, taking Cardpoint's ATM estate to 2,068 machines. Cardpoint was subsequently merged with Alphyra to become Payzone, which now belongs to Duke Street Capital. Today, Mills specialises in helping companies prepare themselves for sale.

Dan Somers

Company: VC-Net
Young Gun in: 2004 (Age: 30)
Dan Somers quickly established VC-Net as a leading provider of global networking video-conferencing technology, a success he puts down to providing the highest quality service that technology can deliver. In 2003, when the business was three years old, its turnover was £1.5m, and he was expecting that to double in 2004, the year he was named a Young Gun. Somers exited VC-Net in 2011, and today focuses on angel investing.

Preet Chahal

Company: ihotdesk
Young Gun in: 2004 (Age: 35)
With a client in the US already lined up, Chahal and David Horwood founded their IT support business in 1999 with around £4,000 worth of investment, making it profitable from day one. By growing purely organically, the company had reached a £1.8m turnover by 2004. Chahal, whose degree was in management and computer sciences, previously worked for J. P. Morgan, Nokia and ABN AMRO in technical and operational positions. He remains with ihotdesk as managing director.

Paul Hawkins

Company: Hawk-Eye Innovations
Young Gun in: 2004 (Age: 30)
Winchester-based Hawk-Eye had only eight employees in 2004 but had made its impact felt already in Test Match cricket and Wimbledon coverage. The ball-tracking technology went on to revolutionise the adjudication process for tennis and cricket, and later football, with FIFA giving authorisation to the firm to install its goal-line technology systems worldwide in late 2012. The firm, which had achieved a turnover of £1.2m in the year when founder Dr Paul Hawkins was named a Young Gun, had started working with Sony by that stage. In March 2011, Hawk-Eye was sold in its entirety to the electronics giant.

Daniel Drury

Company: WebAbacus
Young Gun in: 2004 (Age: 33)
WebAbacus was launched in 2001 as a stand-alone company, and when Drury was hired to run it, he started driving up turnover from day one. The technology identifies the most productive and profitable parts of clients' websites as well as their failing areas. Drury had pedigree, too, having previously set up and run another software business, Cognition Consulting, straight out of university in 1993; he sold this seven years later for £5.3m, just prior to the dotcom collapse. Today, after 12 years

as an internet entrepreneur and angel investor, Drury is working at consultancy group Bowen Craggs as commercial director.

Gary McWilliam

Company: The Hire Supply Company
Young Gun in: 2004 (Age: 34)
McWilliam's Nottinghamshire-based business supplies equipment to the hire industry, which includes gardening, landscaping, site electrical works and climate control. Although it was started in 1995, McWilliam didn't come on board until 2001, taking the business from a £300,000 turnover to £2.7m in three years by revamping its product portfolio. In 2004, revenues reached £3.1m, and they have continued to rise during his time so far as managing director.

Graham Bucknall

Company: Adventi
Young Gun in: 2004 (Age: 33)
Capitalising on the growing trend to outsource, Bucknall set up Edinburgh-based Adventi in 2002 to provide IT support for SMEs in Scotland. 'The aim is to be a £20m turnover company within five years, with 300 staff,' said the ambitious Bucknall in 2004, who was previously brought in to run and raise finance for fund information portal Trustnet. He had grown Adventi into one of Scotland's leading IT consultancy firms by the time he stepped down from his executive position in 2008.

Jef Richards

Company: Galleria RTS
Young Gun in: 2004 (Age: 30)
Retail planning technology business Galleria was already 15 years old in 2004, but after Richards had invested in it and had taken the role of chief technology officer in 2002, the Cheshire-based company had grown to a £3m turnover in 2003 and £4m in 2004. The company remains a leading provider of retail technology solutions, although Richards stepped down as a director in 2012.

Ravi Gehlot

Company: OneOffice
Young Gun in: 2005 (Age: 22)
Gehlot's a fast worker. At 15 he was organising club nights, making £3,000 a time. Next he took his events skills to Cyprus party resort Ayia Napa under the gaze of Channel 4, then returned to put on parties for MTV. At the ripe old age of 20 he launched OneOffice, offering a fully automated virtual office service complete with Mayfair address. By 2005 it had 2,000 clients and was turning over £100,000 a month.

Chris Philp

Company: Clearstone
Young Gun in: 2005 (Age: 29)
Inside six years, Philp built grocery distribution company Blueheath into a £70m AIM-listed business - and by 2005 he was at it again. Having noticed how hard it was at Blueheath to find lorry drivers, Philp set up Clearstone with co-founder Sam Gyimah in 2003 to re-train unemployed or low-income individuals. Although the company went into administration in 2008, Philp took the opportunity to step into the political arena, becoming the Conservative candidate for Hampstead and Kilburn at the 2010 General Election and losing to Glenda Jackson by just 42 votes. He remains at Pluto Capital, a development finance company he co-founded in 2004.

Patrice Barbedette

Company: Jobpartners
Young Gun in: 2005 (Age: 33)
Having launched a customer relationship management product for a global software company, Barbedette applied his master's degree in European business administration and management to form Jobpartners in 2000. Providing software to help corporate clients better manage their people processes and train and retain staff, Barbedette quickly established Jobpartners as a European market leader. In 2005, turnover was predicted to almost double to £5.3m, and notable clients included Nike, Xerox and Boots. In 2011, the business was acquired by Taleo for $38m.

Sheldon Kaye

Company: Eurosimm
Young Gun in: 2005 (Age: 35)
After starting out selling memory solutions to trade, Kaye and co-founder Richard Harris became adept entrepreneurial chameleons, constantly realigning themselves according to their customers' demands, and by 2005 were supplying complete IT solutions. Experimentation with the internet led to the discovery of a flourishing customer base, swelling turnover to £30m. Today, that has increased still further to over £40m, although Kaye stepped out of the business following a management buyout in 2009.

Andrew Michael

Company: Fasthosts
Young Gun in: 2005 (Age: 24)
In 2000, when internet hosting companies were busy chasing big business and building large London data centres, Michael realised how hard it was to find a host for a small business - so he decided to start one himself. In 2005, Fasthosts' clients numbered 800,000 and its turnover had reached £16m, a success Michael put down to understanding the needs of new and small businesses. Whatever he was doing right, he carried on doing it: in 2006, at which point he still owned 75% equity, he sold the business for £61.5m to German company United Internet. Not one to rest on his laurels, he then founded cloud storage firm Livedrive in 2009, which now has over 500,000 paying customers.

Tom Dawes

Company: Aerogistics Group
Young Gun in: 2005 (Age: 29)
Having studied manufacturing engineering and specialising in aerospace at PhD level, as well as developing a supply chain management portal for Airbus, Dawes identified the need for better project management between small parts' suppliers and end users. His company, Aerogistics Group, represented, managed and marketed a cluster of suppliers to larger manufacturers. In 2010 he founded AeroDNA, which is forecasting revenues of £2m in the 12 months from July 2012.

Jonathan Evans

Company: Martinez & Partners
Young Gun in: 2006 (Age: 25)
Having bought Martinez & Partners, Evans set out to increase earnings seven-fold within 10 years before listing the company. By 2006, he was already well on his way - turnover was projected at £15m, with 50% growth since the takeover in 2005. His strategy was to become a quality niche operator - construction and commodity trader firms were targeted, due to the lack of a bespoke service in the industry. The company, still headed up by Evans, today generates healthy profits and specialises in international insurance.

Russell Lux

Company: Luxtech
Young Gun in: 2006 (Age: 29)
By 2006, Lux had come a long way from fly-posting on people's cars in order to publicise his business. Luxtech boasted an impressive array of clients, following a combination of organic and acquisition-based growth. Today it claims to be one of the UK's leading IT managed services specialists in the SME sector. Still involved with Luxtech, Lux has also found time to take on the role of commercial director at telecoms firm teliqo.

Nick Garlick

Company: Nebulas Security
Young Gun in: 2006 (Age: 32)
The increased threat of IT viral attacks made the security software market particularly fierce, but Garlick's Nebulas Security managed to stand out from the crowd in 2006, having amassed more than 200 high-profile clients. Turnover was set to reach £7.5m by 2007. Today it claims to be the UK's largest independent network security specialist.

Rob Hamilton

Companies: Instant Offices Group
Young Gun in: 2006 (Age: 32)
In 2006, Hamilton likened his business to the Expedia of commercial property, with clients able to book premises with vendors across the world. By the time he was named a Young Gun, he had had more than 100,000 clients, ranging from sole traders to government departments. Offices were established in London, Sydney and Miami. In January 2012, Instant, which experienced a revenue increase of 30% to £22m in 2012, secured a £16m investment from private equity firm MML Capital Partners. The London-based firm now works with more than 5,000 businesses every month to provide them with flexible office solutions in over 100 countries. Hamilton oversaw the group's growth until August 2012, when he stood down as CEO, though he remains as a non-executive director and has retained a share in the company.

Laurence Collins

Company: activ8 intelligence
Young Gun in: 2007 (Age: 35)
Set up in 2005, the company pioneered predictive analytics in HR. Its software profiles job candidates, using factors such as personality and previous experience. In 2006 the firm beat 360 others to win a DTI/BT Technology Innovation Award. Client Legal & General increased 'good hires' from 43% to 84%, saving around £10m over three years. The firm also raised £1m through debt financing from the Royal Bank of Scotland, investment from the East Midlands Regional Venture Capital Fund and private individuals, including Egg founder Paul Gratton. Since then, the company, of which Collins is still managing director, has completed further funding rounds, most recently, in 2012, from commercial venture fund manager Midven's Early Advantage Fund as well as from existing investors and new business angels.

Ben Way

Companies: The Rainmakers, Brightstation Ventures, ViaPost, The Horsesmouth
Young Gun in: 2007 (Age: 27)
Serial entrepreneur and technical whiz-kid Ben Way has set up a string of businesses, was on *The Sunday Times* Rich List at 19, has advised the White House on 3G technology, was crowned Entrepreneur of the Year by Gordon Brown, was the technical architect for social mentoring charity The Horsesmouth and sat on the $100m Brightstation Ventures fund for tech start-ups. In 2007 his consulting and corporate venturing business, The Rainmakers, held equity stakes worth around £10m. Today it claims to be one of the world's leading innovation and incubation companies and has worked with the likes of Microsoft, BT and the Ministry of Defence. Way and sister Hermione could recently be seen on US television in a reality show about setting up in Silicon Valley, which covered the launch of their new product, Ignite.

Scott Davies

Company: Million-2-1
Young Gun in: 2007 (Age: 33)
Million-2-1's white-label technology (which is bought by customers who then rebrand it before selling on to their own customers) for interactive lottery, competition and gaming promised a complete audit trail of entries, a guaranteed winner, and billing only for those who entered within the allotted time. The company raised £3m in 2006 and was projecting £4.5m turnover for 2007. In 2009 the company was acquired by IGT for an undisclosed amount.

Tom Allason

Company: eCourier
Young Gun in: 2007 (Age: 26)
Fuelled by frustration when a courier lost 10 tickets, Allason soon discovered that the £1 billion UK market was under-served and fragmented, with the largest player owning a single-digit share. Realising that having people assigning couriers to jobs was an inefficient model, Allason and

business partner Jay Bregman hired a team to build an 'ultra-smart computer'. AIBA (advanced information-based allocation) was born.

The system – which removes the need for human allocation of bookings – connects with couriers' mobile GPS units, which feed back their exact locations every 15 seconds. It knows everything that could impact on delivery time, such as weather, traffic and even customer type, and picks the most suitable driver for the job. It then compares the actual delivery time with its estimation and gets smarter, giving a better and better service. In 2007 the business had raised £8m and grown organically to turn over £7.2m, with a team of over 200. By 2008, eCourier was number six in the UK's fastest growing technology businesses over a five-year period. Allason partially exited that year when TNT acquired a majority stake in the business.

He founded e-commerce delivery solution Shutl in 2009 and launched in 2010, since averaging more than 50% month-on-month sales growth and today serving 70% of the UK, with retailers ranging from Argos to Karen Millen. Expansion to the US beckons following the company's $3.2m fundraising in October 2012.

Gavin Dein

Company: Reward
Young Gun in: 2008 (Age: 32)
Loyalty programmes are nothing new, but Reward took an innovative approach to the concept, removing the need to carry a loyalty card when shopping. Founded in 2001, it also ensures that the rewards are tailored to consumers' interests and spending patterns. The firm's award-winning cardless technology means that no point-of-sale training is required for employees and there's no extra plastic in consumers' wallets. Dein calls this quid pro quo an 'alignment of interest'. Clients come from the banking, charity and sports sectors and have included HSBC, AC Milan, Halfords and Arcadia. By the time Dein was named a Young Gun in 2008, membership had grown to 5 million and turnover was expected to hit £3m. Dein remains at the company today as executive director.

Oli Barrett

Company: Various
Young Gun in: 2008 (Age: 30)
Former Butlins redcoat and serial entrepreneur Oli Barrett is something of a 'go to guy' for both the public and private sectors. Arguably top of his list of social entrepreneurship achievements is the influential Make Your Mark with a Tenner campaign, which sees 10,000 pupils competing to build enterprises in a month with just £10. He also brought speed networking to the UK, took 20 UK web companies to San Francisco to learn from key people in Silicon Valley for Web Mission, and was one of the people behind StartUp Britain, the independent campaigning organisation to support people starting a business.

Kulbir Sohi and Purvinder Tesse

Company: FCL UK
Young Gun in: 2008 (Ages: 35)
FCL coordinates the movement of clients' cargo around the world. It specialises in catering to the logistical needs of small to medium-sized firms, which the founders feel are often neglected by big shipping firms. Set up in 2003 and entirely self-funded, by 2008 it employed 16 staff and had a £5.9m turnover. As companies became more wary of locking themselves into expensive logistics contracts, FCL was able to take advantage by picking up the slack. The business has since become part of the (still privately owned) FCL Group, which also consists of FCL Infrastructure Developments. The last few years have seen significant diversification, and the group is intent on becoming the biggest independent player in the logistics and civil engineering market in the UK.

Nick Bell

Company: Quick.tv
Young Gun in: 2008 (Age: 24)
By the age of only 25, Bell had already set up and exited four businesses, including teenfront.com, the online magazine he founded at the tender age of 14. He achieved a considerable exit three years later, and the Newcastle-based entrepreneur has been busy ever since. Quick.tv, founded in 2006,

provides a business-to-business service for major brands and e-commerce sites looking for interactive video content for their websites. The business, now renamed Quicktvpro, raised £1m in funding from a combination of angel and venture capital sources in 2007. Today, Bell also works at News International as director of digital products.

Max Williams and Damien Tanner

Company: New Bamboo
Young Gun in: 2008 (Ages: 25 and 21)
Horror stories of web projects running over schedule and over budget abound. Enter New Bamboo. Co-founders Tanner and Williams are proponents of a project management style known as Agile, which involves regular meetings with clients to avoid these problems. They are also specialists in a new web development framework, Ruby on Rails; this allows programmers to create well-designed applications more rapidly than they could in Java or .NET. Its clients include Amnesty International and Channel 5.

Dan McGuire

Companies: Broadbean Technology
Young Gun in: 2008 (Age: 27)
McGuire joined Broadbean, set up by serial entrepreneur Kelly Robinson, at 21. He believed in the concept so much that he took out a loan to buy a 25% equity chunk of the business, and ran it successfully on a £35,000 overdraft for the first 24 months. By 2008 it had become a market leader, turning over £3.5m and with offices in London, Amsterdam and LA. Broadbean's innovative technology distributes job ads to multiple locations online and allows recruiters to track their return from online ad spend. Following the sale of Broadbean to Daily Mail and General Trust's digital arm in 2008, McGuire started a visual analytics business in 2011. Officially launched in May 2012 after a £0.5m personal investment, cube19 develops cloud-based graphics that are used to simplify complex data. Having secured funding of $1.75m from private investors in November 2012, McGuire now plans to hit the global staffing and sales markets.

Kate Craig-Wood

Company: Memset
Young Gun in: 2008 (Age: 31)
After leaving a senior position at Easyspace, one of the UK's largest web hosting companies, Craig-Wood formed Memset with her brother Nick in late 2002. Its focus on technology, innovation and corporate social responsibility led to some impressive client wins, including Experian, Hilton and The Disney Store. In 2006, Memset became the first UK internet service provider to be carbon neutral, a move that marked an acceleration in its growth. It has remained debt-free and profitable, and has grown organically, with Kate and Nick holding 90% equity.

Tim Wallis and Craig Beard

Company: Content and Code
Young Gun in: 2008 (Ages: 35)
The disarmingly affable Wallis co-founded Content and Code in 2001 with Craig Beard, and the London-based IT consultancy has been enjoying solid organic growth ever since. In 2008, Wallis attributed the strength of the firm - then turning over £3.5m - to a restructuring that saw him move from the role of chief technology officer to chief executive. Now one of the UK's market leaders in the provision of Microsoft business products, having been a Microsoft Gold Partner since 2003, the company counts Deloitte, Sony, EMI, BT and Virgin Atlantic among its clients.

Stephen Abel

Companies: Parcels4Delivery, Parcel Shipping Manager
Young Gun in: 2008 (Age: 33)
While there are many courier companies, Abel differentiated his offering by developing groundbreaking technology. His Parcels4Delivery business can process an unlimited number of parcel movements per day. In fact, so efficient is his technology that a client could ship a million parcels to a million different addresses and Abel wouldn't even have to get out of bed. As well as licensing his technology to competitors, he is also able to resell courier services from major carriers by integrating with their systems. A separate company, Parcel Shipping Manager (PSM), saves businesses from

having to waste hours typing in their shipping information. The PSM software pulls the data from a firm's shopping cart or an eBay account and sends it to DHL or Parcelforce.

Andrew Long

Company: Ten Lifestyle Management
Young Gun in: 2009 (Age: 33)
Many are the entrepreneurs for whom the mention of banks causes some teeth-gnashing. Andrew Long, co-founder of concierge business Ten Group, is not one of them. Many may have a legitimate beef with banks' reluctance to lend to small businesses, but Long and co-founder Alex Cheatle are in the enviable position of counting large banks among their major clients. And, surprisingly perhaps, at a time that hasn't been the rosiest for the banking world, Ten Group has managed not just to retain the banks' custom but, thanks to a laser-like focus on quality of service alongside smart worldwide expansion, to increase its volume dramatically.

Brothers Long and Cheatle founded their business in 1998: Ten Lifestyle Management, the ultimate service business, based on the promise to do anything its clients didn't have the 'time, expertise or inclination' to do themselves. Back then, concierge businesses were thin on the ground to say the least; now they're ten-a-penny, making Ten's continued position at the front of the pack all the more impressive. By the time Long was named a Young Gun in 2009, Ten Lifestyle Management was managing 25,000 requests a month for more than 300,000 private and corporate members. Its turnover stood at £11.5m, and was expected to double in 2010.

Getting there, however, was not plain sailing. The business went into liquidation in 2003. 'We made poor business decisions,' Long explains. Believing a client when they were told a large contract was coming their way meant they hired a lot of people; but, as Long says, the world changed in 2003 and the contract failed to materialise. The duo shut down the business, but with admirable indefatigability, not to mention a great deal of belief in their venture, they raised funding from friends, family and angel investors and re-launched the service. 'That made us risk averse for quite a while,' says Long, and it's easy to see why.

So perhaps the entrepreneurs would have been forgiven for reining in their ambition, for being content with building a small, well-run, stable firm. Instead, their drive to create a world-changing business remained undimmed. To this end, there are now a few strings to Ten's bow. In 2005, the group launched its professional services division. Currently, this centres on a service for head teachers named The Key. The education sector seems a somewhat unlikely place to find a business specialising in managing requests for wealthy clients, but it was spotted that Ten could easily apply its concierge model to the problems head teachers were facing. At this time, Long explains, there was a real problem with head teacher retention, to the extent that some were worried about there simply not being enough of them within a few years. Research showed that the problem stemmed from the amount of bureaucracy that head teachers were expected to handle, preventing them from doing their jobs as effectively as they would like. The government had responded by sending private consultants to state schools once or twice a year, at huge expense. But Ten realised that every head teacher was facing almost identical challenges, and created an online solution to help them.

In effect, it uses the same level of expertise and research that had made Ten's concierge services so successful, and applies them to head teachers' questions on school leadership and management. The service was quickly taken up by the government, which funded it for two years. But in 2009, government funding across the board dried up, and the service was cut.

We were faced with a big decision. Should we walk away from this? Or are we confident we can make it work as a scalable, commercial enterprise?

Again, one might have expected this to be the end of the road for this element of Ten's business. As Long says: 'We were faced with a big decision. Should we walk away from this? Or are we confident we can make it work as a scalable, commercial enterprise?' Long and Cheatle chose the latter and invested in selling it directly to schools. 'Local authorities are now often buying it for schools in their area,' explains Long, 'much like the way banks buy from us for their clients.'

Today he says, 'in every metric it's improving month on month and is profitable and cash generative, and is outperforming our expectations. It's now got real traction: 20% of UK schools are now signed up to The Key.' Now the model has been proven in the education sector, Long is confident it can be replicated in different sectors, including health.

Ten Group's real focus today, however, is on international expansion of its corporate concierge services; this is the area that generates the vast majority of the group's revenues. To this end, Long has recently relocated to Singapore to take up the role of CEO Asia Pacific. 'Asia has become an important part of the business and where we see the big growth opportunity,' he explains. Today there are offices in Hong Kong, Japan and Singapore – with South Korea and Australia to follow – as well as in Mexico City, Miami, San Francisco and New York.

The ability to expand to such an extent over recent years is due to the banks, which use Ten's services as a benefit for valued customers. According to Long, banks recently decided that concierge services had to be of genuine quality and cost-effectiveness. Ten's competitive advantage, Long says, stems from the fact that it has never been a call centre operation. 'We invested millions in technology and specialists. If you want a restaurant reservation or theatre ticket, you'll speak to someone who used to work in that sector – someone who knows the maître d', for example.' As a result, the big buyers of concierge services, particularly Amex and Citigroup, migrated their portfolios over to Ten. Simultaneously, says Long, other companies are waking up to the idea of concierge services as an effective customer retention tool. 'We have been able to demonstrate that concierge is a profit driver for a bank rather than a cost.' The extent to which this has allowed the business to grow is evidenced by the fact that the business does not launch a new office unless it has won a large contract in the area, thereby removing the risks associated with the expensive process.

The fact that Ten has been ambitious in its international presence has been of particular importance, since the UK market, in concierge services as in so many areas, has been flat of recent years. Says Long: 'We've managed to retain all our top clients ... we haven't seen new contracts going out to tender ... but our real growth through the financial crisis is international. There's been no market in Europe.'

Long has remained very aware of the risks the company has had to navigate – from those posed by newer competitors, as a result of which the company has had to fight harder than ever to win new tenders, to growing too fast and taking their eye off the cash flow – hence the recent appointment of a financial director with FTSE 100 experience.

But there has been no stemming Long's ambition. Ultimately, the founders plan to sell the Ten Group, but not before making it 'the most trusted business in the world', with a turnover of £100m within five years. The growth of this company so far has proved a fascinating journey, but there's lots more to come.

James Taylor

Company: SportStars
Young Gun in: 2009 (Age: 27)
James Taylor started SportStars with £1,000 given to him by his parents on his 21st birthday. He quickly secured five contracts, and by 2009 the business was working with 25,000 children each week in 100 schools, offering sports coaching to cover teachers' planning, preparation and assessment time as well as in the school holidays. The company has since rebranded as SuperStars in order to reflect its diversified services, which now include art and music lessons, after-school clubs and holiday courses. In 2011, the company made its first acquisition with the takeover of Rising Stars, one of its principal competitors.

Nirmal Chhabria

Company: Niva International
Young Gun in: 2009 (Age: 27)
MBA graduate Nirmal Chhabria founded Niva International in 2005. The company focused on scrapping high-quality waste metal and exporting it to China, India and parts of Southern Asia. Mumbai-born Chhabria also founded Niva Global Services, which helps Indian students access higher education in the UK, assisting with everything from finding the right course to admissions, accommodation and travel.

Will Saville and Richard Paterson

Company: BrightStarr
Young Gun in: 2009 (Ages: 33)
IT services firm BrightStarr specialises in providing project collaboration tools for large organisations, with clients including Pepsi, Mulberry and

the NHS. Founded by Will Saville and Richard Paterson in 2006, Bright Starr has a presence in the Middle East, and in New Jersey, Boston and Houston in the US.

Azhar Majid Saddique

Company: UK Equipment Direct
Young Gun in: 2009 (Age: 31)
Azhar Saddique began trading from his bedroom in 2007, after accepting a £2,500 redundancy package from Centrica. With no bank credit or external finance to speak of, the business turned over £1m in its first six months and by 2009 had supplied more than 10,000 organisations, including the NHS. UK Equipment Direct offered a complete one-stop service to the catering industry, covering design and installation. In 2012, Saddique was one of the crop of entrepreneurs hoping to impress Lord Sugar in *The Apprentice*, although ultimately he was on the receiving end of the infamous 'You're fired'. He subsequently left UK Equipment Direct.

Angus Hewlett

Company: FXpansion Audio UK
Young Gun in: 2009 (Age: 32)
Faithless, The Cure and deadmau5 are just a few of the musicians, recording artists, composers, producers and engineers who were using Angus Hewlett's music software by 2009. His products were licensed by 30 companies across the globe, including Avid, Numark and Yamaha, as well as being used by a number of academic institutions and more than 500,000 individuals. FXpansion's BFD 2.0 drum machine software sold 4,000 units during its first three months of release, and many new products have been released since then.

Scott Fletcher

Company: ANS Group
Young Gun in: 2009 (Age: 35)
PLUS Chairman of the Year Scott Fletcher started ANS Group at age 17. The firm, which raised £1.5m on its flotation on junior stock exchange

PLUS in 2000, comprised three other companies by 2009, including Smart Identity, an identity management software development firm founded by Fletcher, and two acquired businesses. The company has experienced 80% year-on-year growth since 2009 and currently turns over £50m. The acquisition of Alpha Business Computers by ANS Group was named Transaction of the Year at the PLUS awards in May 2011.

Matt Waller

Company: Benefex
Young Gun in: 2009 (Age: 34)
In 2009, the employee benefit scheme provider had customers spanning 25 countries and a healthy £1.5m turnover. Today providing services to over 500 customers in 40 countries, Benefex became the first recipient of finance from the Business Growth Fund in 2011, welcoming a £4.2m investment. Expecting a turnover of £10m in 2012, Benefex has used strategic partnerships to expand its services, most recently striking a deal with independent financial advice company Positive Solutions.

Andy Gilbert

Company: Node 4
Young Gun in: 2010 (Age: 29)
Founded in 2004, Derby-based Node 4 was projecting an impressive £10m turnover for 2009-10, saw a £3.4m profit in 2009 and had 34 staff. Not bad going for an entrepreneur who dropped out of school at 16. There's no denying the strength of Andy Gilbert's background in IT, though, as he started his career as a developer involved in projects for clients such as PC World and was a technical director for another IT services provider before founding Node 4. The business opened its third data centre in September 2012 and currently turns over approximately £11m.

Daniel Lowe

Company: UKSolutions
Young Gun in: 2010 (Age: 31)
When Daniel Lowe first started presenting to large companies in his late teens, he struggled to be taken seriously - it was often easier for him to

pretend to be an employee rather than the managing director of his company. However, by 2009, UKSolutions was turning over more than £4m. The company specialised in hosting valuable data for clients of all sizes, which is stored in a unit that makes Fort Knox look low security. His business weathered the recession admirably, and in 2011 it was acquired by Six Degrees, where Lowe remains as part of the senior management team.

Jamie Waller

Company: JBW Group
Young Gun in: 2010 (Age: 31)

As far as challenges go, Jamie Waller set himself a difficult one when he founded JBW in 2004. He faced the challenge not merely of growing a successful, sustainable and industry-leading business - though that's no cakewalk - but of transforming the public perception of the bailiff industry. Estate agents, politicians, journalists ... bailiffs could easily sit on this list of much-maligned professionals. But this is unfair, as Waller has pointed out: the industry is a necessary one, and, thanks largely to his efforts, it is one that has become more transparent, ethical and innovative.

An ex-bailiff himself, Waller was only 22 when he co-founded his own business. In a stroke of luck, the BBC approached him about appearing in a fly-on-the-wall documentary; *Bailiffs* went on to attract 9 million viewers, giving the business publicity most start-ups can only dream of. However, Waller left this company to start from scratch all over again - this time entirely on his own - and thanks to clients following him, JBW grew quickly. By the time Waller was named a Young Gun in 2010, the business had survived the recession, coming out 'leaner and stronger' with a turnover of more than £7m.

Furthermore, it had successfully completed two acquisitions: Darlington-based National Enforcement Services was bought in March 2010, and in July that year JBW acquired Hammond Hillman, a business based in Southend-on-Sea, adding 10 new clients and 22 staff to the business and making it the largest provider of bailiff services in the south-east. Waller describes both these acquisitions as strategically important in terms of both geography and sector.

Since then, arguably the most important development for the company has been the development of its proprietary technology, namely a debt recovery solution known as AR-12. Since day one, Waller has been technology- and innovation-focused in an industry not known for its forward thinking. In keeping with this, the company has created its own technology, based on the systems used by Addison Lee to impressive effect. Within months of rolling it out, it had delivered an increase of around 50% in bailiff productivity, as well as around 8% more revenue collected for clients and reduced fees for debtors, according to JBW. AR-12 is now being offered to government departments and debt recovery businesses. Waller has high hopes, predicting that 'AR-12 will reduce the size of the industry and increase the success of comparative industries like debt recovery for consumer debt'. He also anticipates that it will 'deliver a consistent, compliant service which the UK government will want to see across their entire debtor portfolio'.

The launch of this business has been a highlight of 2012, says Waller, along with the rather impressive statistic that JBW has won all of the public sector contracts for which it has tendered. Other highlights since being named a Young Gun include the company being named in *The Sunday Times* Best Companies to Work For list two years in a row, surely a sign that Waller is succeeding in his efforts to banish the old associations of the bailiff industry. Rather than the ex-doormen of old, Waller realised from the start that successful bailiffs have the same skill set as sales-people, and hired accordingly.

> **We invest in research and development all of the time and have people dedicated to this.**

Today, the turnover of JBW stands at £16m, with year-on-year growth of approximately 20%. Waller credits this growth to investment in staff, word-of-mouth referral from happy clients, and constant innovation. 'We have been the only company in our sector to deliver new products and services consistently since formation,' says Waller. 'We invest in research and development all of the time and have people dedicated to this.' Next year, he is focused on achieving 30% organic growth, and finding his next acquisition target. One option is a reverse takeover – the company now has the technology, says Waller, to allow it to acquire a £25m plus company. Such an acquisition would take this mould-breaking firm to the next level. Watch this space.

Daniel Ox

Company: Fruit for the Office
Young Gun in: 2010 (Age: 30)
Selling his flat to finance Fruit for the Office might have been a risky move, but it paid off for Daniel Ox, whose business was formed to deliver fresh fruit to office workers throughout London. He was certainly not the only person to see the potential in desk-bound wage slaves, but he's stayed ahead of the pack and diversified into the catering industry to ensure the continued growth of the business. It now also sells vegetables and fruit to hotels and restaurants through its website – a less saturated market that is worth around £2 billion in the UK, according to Ox. By introducing a technology platform, Ox has taken a significant step in bringing a very traditional industry up to date.

Mitesh Patel

Company: Fifosys
Young Gun in: 2010 (Age: 32)
Fifosys was set up in 2001 to provide a 'link between IT and business with a personal touch' when founder Mitesh Patel was studying for his MSc in Computer Science. Key services include cloud computing, tailored IT support, budget planning, auditing and project management. Since 2010, Patel has almost doubled the company's turnover through its 2011 acquisition of Octavia Information Systems.

Neal Harrison

Company: Convergence Group
Young Gun in: 2010 (Age: 35)
From road digger to chief executive of a multimillion-pound company, Neal Harrison's entrepreneurial journey has been an impressive one. He's hoping for big things from his Midlands-based IT and telecommunications company, which designs and builds corporate data networks.

Wesley Downham and Peter Harrison

Company: FGH Security
Young Gun in: 2010 (Ages: 32 and 27)
Venturing into the *Dragons' Den* in 2010 proved to be a canny business decision from Peter Harrison and Wesley Downham, who received offers from all five Dragons and left with £100,000 from Peter Jones and Theo Paphitis. The business was already established, though, providing services ranging from door security to CCTV installation. With over 3,000 clients, including the NHS, Revolution Vodka Bars, local councils and the Subway franchises, the business is growing both organically and through acquisitions.

Heather Wilkinson

Company: Striding Out
Young Gun in: 2011 (Age: 32)
Social enterprise Striding Out Community Interest Company was founded by Heather Wilkinson in 2005 when she was only 26. Today it works with individuals of all ages and backgrounds to help them achieve their potential – providing leadership, business and career coaching services that are supported by training, networking and work placement. In 2010 alone it generated revenues of £1.3m and supported 4,000 individuals across the UK. Says Wilkinson: 'My vision was for Striding Out to operate on a national scale with the support of a network of coaches and in 2010 I really felt we had taken a large step towards achieving this milestone.' By the time Wilkinson was a 2011 Young Gun, the business was operating in six UK regions and was aiming to expand its services to all parts of the UK, and to grow its turnover to £5m by 2014.

Emma Sinclair

Company: Target Parking
Young Gun in: 2011 (Age: 29)
Many people would be delighted to secure a high-powered City job, with a hefty salary and jet-setting lifestyle, by the age of 27. But, for Emma Sinclair, this wasn't enough; she wanted to chase her entrepreneurial dream. The youngest person to float a company on AIM, at 29, she

identified a gap in the car park sector when she bought a small car parking firm. Now on her second car park business, she has set about turning Target Parking, a company that currently boasts an array of clients from DTZ to Urban Splash to the Forestry Commission Scotland, into a major force.

The business, which offers a range of services to Britain's car parks including management, security, cash handling and facilities management, has successfully managed over 450 sites across the UK for private and public clients. In June 2012, Target Parking added Wolverhampton Wanderers to its client bank following a lucrative deal to manage the stadium car parks. Recently appointed as a *Telegraph* Wonder Woman, Sinclair shares her business knowledge in a weekly column.

Matt Miller

Company: ustwo
Young Gun in: 2012 (Age: 34)
Started by 'Mills & Sinx' - or Matt Miller and John Sinclair - in 2004, ustwo has quickly become the UX/UI digital design studio of choice. The London-based company has worked with the likes of Sony, Sony Ericsson, H&M, Channel 4 and Barclays to develop multi-platform digital experiences, products and user interfaces.

The business employs 120 staff and has opened studios in London, Malmö (Sweden) and recently New York. Miller has found that designing ustwo-branded apps alongside client work is effective marketing, and has helped create a devoted user base of millions along the way. The company is predicting a £10.5m turnover in 2013.

Ben Donnelly

Company: Elixir Group
Young Gun in: 2012 (Age: 34)
Recycling specialist Elixir Group is much more ambitious than its area of expertise - waste management - might suggest. As a social enterprise, it is committed to providing employment and training for vulnerable adults and socially excluded groups, such as ex-prisoners and recovering addicts. Co-founder Ben Donnelly was recovering from addictions himself

in 2008 when he realised that there was a lack of support for people in similar situations coming out of rehab or prison. Elixir Group was born and has successfully employed over 800 vulnerable adults. Its clients are a range of private and public sector companies, and the business has reached a decidedly healthy turnover.

Erich Wasserman

Company: MediaMath
Young Gun in: 2012 (Age: 35)
With 130% year-on-year growth over the past five years, MediaMath is the world's leading provider of digital media trading technology to marketers. This innovative company, co-founded by British-born Wasserman in 2007, invented the demand side platform (DSP). The DSP enables marketers to target and optimise advertising inventory in real time across automated media markets. It is also the fastest growing sector of online advertising and has attracted every major agency holding group, as well as brands that include American Express, General Mills, Kayak and MoneySupermarket. As the joint head of the company's EMEA (Europe, Middle East and Africa) and APAC (Asia Pacific) operations, Wasserman has established a presence in the European market from headquarters in London, with seven additional offices worldwide.

Consumer services

Tony Rafferty

Company: Printing.com
Young Gun in: 2003 (Age: 35)
Organising club nights at university and producing flyers for them contributed to Rafferty failing his degree. That isn't something he is likely to spend too much time worrying about today, however. As the CEO of an AIM-listed printing firm worth around £20m, he has his hands more than full. Especially since, at a time when the printing industry as a whole has struggled, Rafferty has managed to find ways of developing and innovating to ensure that Printing.com has not just survived but thrived.

Tony Rafferty was one of the first ever Young Guns in 2003 when his Manchester-based printing and franchise company already employed 110 staff and was looking to hit a turnover of £10m in the next financial year. He had successfully taken the firm to OFEX (the forerunner of PLUS) and had become profitable to the tune of £450,000. The business's franchise model was started only a year earlier, in 2002, but before long there were around 280 franchises operating successfully. In 2004, he took the business to AIM. However, says Rafferty, the company didn't get quite as big as he hoped. Today he believes it was because the company wasn't innovating as much as it could have done. He is in no danger of making that mistake twice.

In the years to come, Printing.com would flourish and become a highly successful franchise business. Today it has 267 outlets, of which only six are owned directly. Turnover grew by more than £4m a year to £21.7m by March 2012, with EBITDA (earnings before interest, taxes, depreciation and amortisation) year-on-year growth a healthy 19.9%, rising to £3.4m.

This has not been an easy achievement. The economic downturn led to the demise of many businesses in the printing industry. Rafferty credits the company's focus on proprietary software for a large part of its success, due to the tools the franchises are provided with: 'If we can speed up processes for the franchise partners, that makes it easier for us to stay in the game.' Added to the woes of the economic environment was the fact that the industry was, like many others, having to adapt to the digital age. This shift online, combined with the recession, meant that many businesses failed. Companies that in 2003, says Rafferty, it would have been difficult to imagine folding within a few years were ignobly forced out of business.

Despite the dotcom in its name, in essence Printing.com used to be an offline company. Determined his company wasn't going to be among the legions of failing dinosaurs, Rafferty has placed innovation at the forefront of the company's priorities. From 2008, one of the most important questions the company grappled with was how it was going to add an online component to the business and develop the franchise network into a hybrid online/offline model.

The answer, at least partly, was to use crowdsourcing. Inspired by online photo libraries, through which photographers can upload their images so that they can be used by people such as graphic designers, Printing.com built a system that allowed graphic designers to connect with small business owners who wanted to buy their work. Prior to this, existing template solutions that allowed the end clients to personalise work online didn't meet the requirements of smaller firms, according to Rafferty.

So, in 2012, he launched TemplateCloud, where freelance graphic designers can upload their designs, set their own price and get royalties every time their template is sold online. His aim is to create 'the largest library of online editable design'. Other companies are also able to buy and integrate TemplateCloud; Printing.com is therefore moving from being purely a printing franchise company to also being one that licenses its systems and its content.

Carrying out such a shift as a public company has its challenges, admits Rafferty. 'It's difficult to evolve a new business model in the gaze of the public arena,' he says. 'It would be easier to be private equity backed at the moment, but we are what we are.' Pressure to domicile the new IP in friendlier environs also came from shareholders, but resisting this pressure, Rafferty says, was made much easier by the enhancement of research and development (R&D) tax credits.

Printing.com has built a strong international presence over the last few years. Primarily, this has been achieved by the 2010 acquisition of Media Facility Group BV, a print supplier to the Dutch and Belgian markets that sold direct to the end client rather than through franchises and that was turning over around €6m annually. The €2m acquisition increased the company's activities in the Eurozone, and this has been key in keeping the company's finances healthy during the recession. Sales from franchise channels (in the UK, Ireland and France) were 'challenging' in 2011-12, according to the company, 'reflecting not only the economic situation but also increased online competition'. The fact that, in that year, turnover increased by 27.9% to £21.77m reflected revenue growth from Belgium, and the contribution of the MFG acquisition. Importantly, it also kick-started the company's online move, says Rafferty. 'We knew there were skill sets we didn't have. We also knew we needed to be a bigger business.' The acquisition provided this opportunity and allowed the company to move forward with its new strategy.

> **We knew there were skill sets we didn't have. We also knew we needed to be a bigger business.**

Unsurprisingly, given its potential value to the company, Rafferty is focused on taking TemplateCloud into international territories too. The US represents a large opportunity, and it will also be launched in countries including Sweden, Spain, France, Italy and Portugal. 'This is a competitive advantage we have to leverage quickly,' says Rafferty. 'We need to exploit what we've developed.'

This is an exciting time for Printing.com as it moves from development to monetisation. 'There's a lot of energy in the company at the moment,' says Rafferty, showing how a large, successful, even public company can retain and reap the advantages of a start-up's willingness to adapt and evolve.

James Keay

Company: Select-a-skip
Young Gun in: 2003 (Age: 31)
Keay's former employer at a skip hire company pooh-poohed his suggestion that the company should go nationwide, so he decided to start from scratch. To make ends meet he worked evening shifts at Little Chef for £3 an hour. By 2003, Shrewsbury-based Select-a-skip turned over around £10m a year, and, as managing director, Keay presides over a UK network of skips.

Martin Jones

Company: Freedom Direct
Young Gun in: 2003 (Age: 31)
Jones worked for his parents' travel business only because a job at the local jobcentre fell through at the last minute. He oversaw its sale to a Bank of Scotland-headed consortium three years later after he'd worked his way up from admin clerk on £6,000 a year. Unfortunately for him he was not a beneficiary, and with no income he threw caution to the wind and decided to start his own independent leisure travel agency in his home city, Newcastle. He convinced the bank to give him a £100,000 loan by saying he'd generate £40m in five years. Six years later, Freedom Direct had a turnover of £42m and 165 staff. However, the company closed its doors in 2009.

John Chasey

Company: Iomo
Young Gun in: 2004 (Age: 33)
By 2004, Hampshire-based Iomo had developed a number of high-profile games, including Bafta-nominated *Scooby Doo*, plus *Tomb Raider*, *Thunderbirds* and *Tiger Woods' PGA Tour Golf*. With 25 staff, turnover had reached £1.7m. The company continued to grow and was rebranded Metismo, and bought by Software AG in 2011. Chasey stayed on as a director.

Jennifer Irvine

Company: Pure Package
Young Gun in: 2005 (Age: 29)
Pure Package customers have their entire dietary intake produced by a chef and delivered to their door. By 2005, Irvine's customers included busy, health conscious dieters and celebrities including Linford Christie and Ruby Wax, and turnover had reached £500,000 in little over a year. Today, Irvine remains at the helm and turnover is around the £2m mark.

Ed Bartlett

Company: IGA Worldwide
Young Gun in: 2005 (Age: 29)
A video game developer with 12 years' experience, Bartlett started Bristol-based Hive Partners in 2003, writing brands such as Red Bull into the storylines of major global console games. However, Bartlett spotted problems with the longevity and flexibility of the business model, as brands had to be hard-coded for a game's entire lifespan. So in 2005 Bartlett negotiated the merger of Hive into the newly formed IGA Worldwide, becoming an equal equity co-founder. In 2006 he was instrumental in raising a $17m Series A venture capital round for the company - one of the largest early stage investments in the world that year. He went on to build the foundations of its industry-leading Radial Network, securing landmark inventory deals with firms such as Electronic Arts, Valve, Sega, Atari and Codemasters. Bartlett left the company in 2010 and went on to found The Future Tense, which offers hands-on support and guidance for emerging contemporary artists.

Wesley Cornell

Company: Shopcall
Young Gun in: 2005 (Age: 23)
In 2005, Cornell was looking to profit from the shoppers most companies are ignoring - those who don't want to buy online. Cornell's Coventry-based Shopcall delivered the shopping basket functionality of an e-commerce system over the telephone. It was on course for first year turnover of £2m, but ultimately the venture proved unsuccessful.

James Day

Company: Urban Golf
Young Gun in: 2005 (Age: 24)
Day left school at 18 to join the golf pro circuit and coach at his local club. Frustrated by being unable to practise at night and in bad weather, Day developed the idea of taking golf indoors. Sourcing simulation machines from the US and funding from several of the bankers he coached, Urban Golf opened in Soho in September 2004, offering virtual play for £40 an hour. The concept has proved extremely popular and Day has now opened three clubs in London.

Emma Barnett

Company: Essential Escapes
Young Gun in: 2005 (Age: 31)
Barnett's former publishing employers should have expected that if they sent her exploring the world's greatest spa hotels she would get a taste for it. That's what happened, and, in 2002, along with solicitor sister Deborah (age 33) and private equity entrepreneur Jonathan Brod, she started Essential Escapes, the UK's first dedicated luxury spa operator. Organic growth saw the company hit the £1m annual turnover mark by 2005, a figure that has since trebled. Barnett also launched Tots Too in 2007, specialising in luxury resorts and hotels for families.

Ella Heeks

Company: Abel & Cole
Young Gun in: 2005 (Age: 27)
When founders decide to bring in management, most look to experienced 'been there, done that' business leaders. Abel & Cole recruited 22-year-old Heeks fresh out of university. After five years, in 2005, losses had been replaced by healthy profit and its £500,000 turnover had grown to £14m. Heeks installed professional internal structures, but insisted that the key factor had been her refusal to compromise the organic food delivery company's principles of providing a personal, human and committed service to both its customers and growers. The company had become Britain's leading organic home delivery company by the time she left Abel & Cole, and Heeks went on to help other entrepreneurs with her advice and public speaking.

Sarah McVittie

Company: RE5ULT
Young Gun in: 2005 (age: 27)
McVittie was at the vanguard of a new service when she co-founded RE5ULT, later rebranded as Texperts, the world's first text messaging answering service. It won numerous awards for its concept and technology, and was sold to KGB, owners of the 118118 directory enquiries service, in a multimillion-pound deal in 2008. Since then she has gone on to co-found Dressipi, the free fashion advice and recommendation service.

Jennie Johnson

Company: Kids Allowed
Young Gun in: 2006 (Age: 34)
Perplexed by the inflexible nature of many nurseries, Johnson decided it was high time she set up her own, Kids Allowed, which incorporates a myriad of services, such as after-school and holiday care for under-10s, dry cleaning and laundry. Johnson secured £5m in funding from a property developer, who built the first two purpose-made Kids Allowed centres in 2005. In 2012, work started on the fifth centre in the north-west, and turnover for the year is predicted to hit £6.2m.

Ben Drury

Company: 7digital
Young Gun in: 2006 (Age: 30)
Founded in 2004, 7digital's indiestore.com made a name for itself by offering unsigned bands the chance to showcase and sell their music, with sales counting towards the UK and US charts. More than 680 bands signed up within the first 48 hours, with video and other downloads onto different formats offered by Drury before iTunes got there. Today, the company claims to be the world's leading open music platform, and is partnered with tech firms including Toshiba, Samsung and HTC. It sold a 50% share to HMV in 2009, but says the recent demise of the retailer will have 'no material impact' on the business. Largely this is due to a $10m deal Drury signed with a strategic media partner prior to the company's collapse, which reduced HMV to a minority shareholder. In November 2012, it raised a £10m investment from strategic technology partners, with which Drury plans to expand beyond music downloads, adding on-demand streaming, radio and scan-and-match products to 7digital's services. Growth plans also include expansion into Europe and North America. The investment coincided with a new contract with RIM, which will make 7digital the official music download provider for the BlackBerry 10 smartphones, due to be launched in 2013. In August 2012, Drury was named in *Billboard*'s prestigious '40 under 40' list, which honours rising young executives pushing the industry forward.

Pepita Diamand

Company: Wrapit
Young Gun in: 2006 (Age: 34)
In 2006, Diamand described her business as 'the best wedding gift list service in Britain'. The virtual department store and 14 showrooms across the UK were on track to draw in an estimated 200,000 users by the end of the year, boosting turnover to £7.5m from 2005's £5m figure. Sadly, however, the company, which had grown to become Britain's third largest gift list service, went bankrupt in 2009. The business failed to make money, despite its impressive growth, and reportedly owed HSBC £3.5m when it collapsed.

Nichola Lawton

Company: DNA Clinics
Young Gun in: 2007 (Age: 28)
Biomolecular science graduate and former Shell Livewire winner Nichola Lawton set up the UK's first DNA clinic in Liverpool in 2004. The company was dissolved in 2007.

Nick Robinson

Company: World First
Young Gun in: 2007 (Age: 33)

Sometimes it's the simplest things that can set a business apart in an extremely crowded market. If, for example, customers have to usually wait a week for the service your business intends to provide, then it makes sense to provide a high-speed alternative. World First has done exactly that, and its customers can make international money transfers much faster than if they were using a bank. Thanks largely to this, and to its resolutely service-led ethos, co-founders Nick Robinson and Jonathan Quin have created a business that, despite its legions of heavy-weight competitors, has become a giant in its field.

The signs were there in 2007, when World First was only three years old and Robinson was named a Young Gun. Posting £1m profit on a £3m turnover, it's perhaps no surprise that it had already secured investment from Prudential chairman and former deputy governor of the Bank of England Sir David Clementi, who remains on the business's board today. It had already transacted with more than 10,000 private clients and 1,000 companies, and was competing with banks on both service and rates. By the end of that year, the company had completed over £1 billion worth of transactions.

Fast-forward to 2013. A forecast turnover of £3.7 billion and profit of £5.35m in the 2012–13 financial year; the fact that it is the UK's leading foreign exchange broker; a rapidly expanding global presence – World First is delivering on its promise.

These are exciting times for the company. In September 2012 it launched World First USA with the opening of an office in Washington DC, a development that represents a huge opportunity for the company. Competition in North America is thin on the ground, Robinson explains, as a result of regulation that came into force post 9/11.

'Typically, individuals and small- to medium-sized businesses get very poor exchange rates from the US banks,' says Robinson, 'and international payments from the US banks can take days to reach their destination.'

World First therefore allows customers – both private individuals and corporate clients – to access better exchange rates, make speedy international payments and receive the kind of personalised support that the big banks reserve for a select few top-tier clients. The aim is no less than to 'transform foreign exchange services in the US'. Examples of the kind of

The entire company ethos is based on placing the client experience at the centre of the business.

customer service that gives World First the edge over its competitors include ensuring that clients always speak to a human being, rather than an automated service, and that the phone is always answered within three rings. Simple things, yes, but remarkably effective; in 2010 the firm won Service Business of the Year in the Fast Growth Business Awards, and it was awarded a National Business Award for customer focus in

November 2012, with co-founder Jonathan Quin commenting: 'It's fitting that we've won in the "customer focus" category because the entire company ethos is based on placing the client experience at the centre of the business.'

The company's method of doing this is to encourage employee feedback. Says Robinson: 'We encourage all staff to come up with ideas to improve the service or World First experience for our clients. We receive tens of new ideas every week and they are prioritised accordingly.'

The US operation isn't the first international presence the company has established. Robinson himself moved to Sydney for a few years to launch the Australian office in 2008, since which time, he says: 'The business in the southern hemisphere has gone from strength to strength.' Recently, an Australian managing director was hired to oversee the growth of the territory. The idea behind these offices was to give World First an 'around the clock' offering, with Sydney, London and Washington DC allowing the business to provide a 24-hour service to clients, regardless of their location.

The company's innovation doesn't lie solely with its customer focus, however. It has made a name for itself by bringing alternative hedging strategies to the SME arena. Granted Financial Services Authority (FSA) approval in 2008, it became the first foreign exchange broker in the UK to be able to sell currency options.

Despite its fast growth – World First has been named among the UK's fastest growing businesses in *The Sunday Times* Fast Track 100 for three consecutive years – the company's expansion has been 100% organic, funded through retained profits. And today, says Robinson, understatedly, 'more growth is the plan'. This will centre largely on World First USA, but, he says, 'we hope to expand our client base in all our offices'. He is also looking to develop further the company's use of technology, thereby automating many of the processes that are currently done manually. Happily, Robinson says: 'This will not result in staff losses but will negate the need for aggressive hiring in the UK office as we have done since we started.'

World First is an impressive business in many ways. Even its staff retention is unusual: by the end of its second year (2005), for example, the company had eight members of staff; seven remain with the firm today. Robinson is justifiably proud that so many of the business's early employees now run large parts of World First, and the company has been listed by *The Sunday Times* as being among the best UK companies to work for. Robinson and Quin have taken a relatively straightforward idea, but the way in which they have executed it is a lesson in sustainable growth for many an aspiring entrepreneur.

Perhaps the clearest indicator of the company's success so far, and its potential overseas, is the fact that in a survey in 2011, a full 100% of World First's clients said they would use the business again and recommend it to friends.

William Davies and Nick Bizley

Company: Aspect Maintenance
Young Gun in: 2008 (Ages: 34 and 33)
Founded in 2005, Aspect Maintenance offers a full range of property repair services, with work evenly balanced between pre-booked jobs and emergency call-outs. Davies, who has a background in investment banking and private equity, helped business partner and friend Nick Bizley, who specialises in maintenance, take a faltering £500,000 firm out of a company voluntary arrangement (CVA) and by 2008 turn it into a profitable £7m business with 115 staff by improving processes and implementing a solid management structure. Turnover today stands at over £10m.

Balthazar Fabricius

Company: Fitzdares
Young Gun in: 2008 (Age: 29)
Priding itself on the ability to offer a tailored service for the 'discerning gambler', Fitzdares prioritises discretion and boasts the best odds. New members are welcomed through word-of-mouth referrals so as to preserve the members' club-style of exclusivity that it offers to big spenders who want to have a flutter. Fabricius had the idea while working at Ladbrokes, where he noticed that the high-street bookies were becoming increasingly comfortable with guaranteed low-margin products. During the 18 months before Fabricius was made a Young Gun, Fitzdares turned a £5m profit on a £89m turnover. In 2011, the business moved into financial spread betting.

Adam Goodyer and James Perkins

Company: Concert Live
Young Gun in: 2008 (Ages: 30)
The initial idea sounded niche enough to put off the Dragons, but recording live music events and selling CDs and downloads to gig-goers obviously has more legs than the TV entrepreneurs envisaged. The concept has proved popular with music fans and the business works with an impressive list of artists. The founding pair has also set up personalised CD store MixPixie.

Alistair Powell

Company: 7CI (Seven Continent Investment)
Young Gun in: 2008 (Age: 26)
Powell always had an interest in property, and made a tidy profit from a website design agency targeting estate agents that he founded when he was just 15. Despite becoming Hamptons International's youngest ever sales manager, he felt true progress would only come from building something of his own. He founded global investment specialist 7CI in 2006 to help high-net-worth individuals buy property abroad, but the venture ultimately failed.

Peter Leiman and Cameron Ogden

Company: Blink
Young Gun in: 2009 (Ages: 30 and 31)
Launching 'Europe's first air taxi service' in the midst of a catastrophic downturn for aviation might sound counterintuitive. However, Blink's promise of the speed, efficiency and comfort of a personal jet at a price that compares with business class was compelling enough to help founders Peter Leiman and Cameron Ogden raise $30m of equity funding in 2007. Based in London, Blink maintains hubs in London, Geneva and the Channel Islands.

Crispin Moger

Company: Young Marmalade
Young Gun in: 2009 (Age: 34)
The confusingly named Young Marmalade is not a rival to Fraser Doherty's SuperJam, but rather an ingeniously simple business that combines car purchase with low-cost vehicle insurance, getting new drivers behind the wheel of safer cars quickly and cost-effectively. Users choose a new or used car on the website, apply for finance, pay a deposit and choose a colour. They then sign the finance papers and a fully insured car is delivered to them. As BBC *Top Gear*'s Richard Hammond said: 'crazy name, clever idea'. Founded by Crispin Moger in 2005, in 2011 annual group sales passed £3.5m.

Christian Arno

Company: Lingo24
Young Gun in: 2009 (Age: 30)
Lingo24 was founded as an online translation company by Oxford University languages graduate Christian Arno from his parents' Aberdeen home in September 2001. The company launched its New Zealand operation in 2003, followed by China in 2004, Romania in 2005, Panama in early 2008 and Edinburgh later the same year. In 2011, Lingo24 opened an Asian hub in Cebu City, the Philippines. Today one of the fastest growing translation companies in the world, the company employs over 150 staff.

Alexandra Burns

Company: For Your Eyes Only Portraits
Young Gun in: 2009 (Age: 35)
A photographic studio that offers makeover portraits might sound like the epitome of a lifestyle business, but Alexandra Burns' For Your Eyes Only Portraits has grown quickly. Burns, a former freelance photographer, was inspired by a vision to give real women access to glamorous 'boudoir-style' portraits, with celebrity style treatment, in the safety of a female-based studio. Her marketing nous helped attract coverage from BBC One, Reuters and Radio 4.

Ali Clabburn

Company: liftshare
Young Gun in: 2009 (Age: 34)
Ali Clabburn's social enterprise liftshare gives businesses the online journey-matching tools to set up their own car-sharing schemes, then helps firms to manage and market them. The idea attracted interest from some major organisations, and by 2009 liftshare could count giants BT, Sony and Tesco among its clients. liftshare now claims to be the world's most successful car-sharing service, and runs over 600 liftshare schemes for communities and businesses. Membership hit 450,000 in 2011, and liftshare currently saves 80,000 car journeys a day.

Tom Marchant, James Merrett and Matt Smith

Company: Black Tomato
Young Gun in: 2009 (Ages: 30)
If you're the kind of person whose idea of a perfect holiday is hunting anacondas in the Brazilian jungle, or going to the hippest bar in town that's only just opened, then Black Tomato is the place for you. Tom Marchant, James Merrett and Matt Smith's business creates bespoke holidays for travellers looking for the inside track on how to experience destinations as the locals do. In 2010 it was included in *The Sunday Times* Fast Track 100 league table, with sales growth of more than 75% a year. The founders have branched out from their original offering, and Black Tomato is now part of the Magnetic Group, which also comprises Beach Tomato, Beach Tomato Shack, Epic Tomato and PINCH magazine.

Karen Hastings

Company: Cupcake
Young Gun in: 2010 (Age: 35)
In 2009, UK birth rates hit a high not seen since 1973, making Hastings' decision to open a members' club for new mums in 2005 a timely one. Cupcake now has three branches in London's Putney, Parsons Green and Wandsworth, where mums, pregnant women and their families can

socialise, attend seminars or take part in fitness classes. The concept of having a spa and crèche in one place has proved popular and much of the angel investment Hastings has received has come from the club's members; however, the six-figure funding for the third centre, opened in 2011, came from Addidi, the UK's first female-only business angel investment firm. Hastings plans to expand even further through franchising, aiming for five new sites in the next five years.

Nicko Williamson

Company: Climatecars
Young Gun in: 2010 (Age: 29)
In 2011, Williamson became the Ernst & Young Entrepreneur of the Year for London and the south-west. Turnover for his eco-friendly cab company had broken £2m, and was running at close to £4m in 2012, with one of the world's largest investment banks as a client. The taxi company is the first to launch 100% electric cars in its 100 plus fleet and has recently launched a booking app. Williamson, who appeared as a mentor on the BBC's *Be Your Own Boss*, aims to hit a turnover of over £10m as quickly as possible.

Will Orr-Ewing

Company: Keystone Tutors
Young Gun in: 2012 (Age: 27)
Orr-Ewing is making a name for his private tutoring company by focusing on professionalism in an area not known for that quality. Only 21 when he founded Keystone Tutors in 2006, the former Harrovian and Oxford graduate has 200 tutors working for him, all of whom have been through a rigorous interview process and are paid a competitive salary. His 'supertutors' include a polar explorer, an amateur boxing champion, and the winner of the 2009 Edinburgh Comedy Award for best newcomer. Displaying 100% year-on-year growth since 2006, the business recorded a turnover of just under £2m in 2011.

Financial services

Mayank Patel

Company: Currencies Direct
Young Gun in: 2003 (Age: 35)
Patel and a now-departed partner launched Currencies Direct in 1996 with £9,000 pooled together to sign a lease on a tiny office in Paddington. By 2002 it was turning over £400m, making the company, which provides finance by phone for major transactions overseas, such as properties, business and migration, one of the UK's fastest growing companies. Today his holding group, Azibo Holdings, comprises Currencies Direct Ltd, Tor Currency Exchange Ltd (TorFx) and Universal VAT Services (USA). Operations are spread across the UK, Spain, France, Portugal, India and South Africa, and Currencies Direct and TorFX have a combined annual turnover of £2.2 billion. In the 2011 Queen's Birthday Honours, Patel was appointed an Officer of the Order of the British Empire (OBE) for his services to financial services and entrepreneurship.

Jason Butler

Company: Jump
Young Gun in: 2004 (Age: 33)
Headhunted and made partner by accountants J. Rothschild by the age of 21, Butler spotted a gap in the market for young house-hunters unable to afford deposits and had set up Homestarter Group in Leeds by the time he was 22. By 2003, it had been taken over by Jump. Butler remained as managing director and a 77.5% shareholder, and turnover to April 2004 was £147.5m. Sadly, the company went into administration in 2005.

Stacey-Lea Golding

Company: Premier Cru
Young Gun in: 2004 (Age: 30)
Golding, who at the age of 19 became the youngest qualified sales associate for J. Rothschild Associates, quit the City to go into business with her mother in 1995. Started specifically to offer structured and manageable investments to people with little or no experience of fine wine, by 2004 Golding had grown Premier Cru into Europe's leading fine wine investment house, and she remains there today as investments director.

Mark Onyett

Company: TDX Group
Young Gun in: 2005 (Age: 33)
Launched in 2003, TDX Group had made fast progress in the financial services market by the time Onyett was named a 2005 Young Gun. Offering a new approach to consumer debt management, working as an intermediary between creditors, debtors and debt collection agencies, TDX Group applies advanced analytics and integrated market knowledge to ensure better collection rates. First year turnover of £1.1m has now grown to approximately £25m. Although Onyett stood down as CEO in 2011, he remains an executive director.

Neil Hutchinson

Company: TrafficBroker/Forward
Young Gun in: 2008 (Age: 30)
Neil Hutchinson was named a Young Gun in 2008, thanks to the breathtaking transformation of his business from one-man band to one of the UK's largest affiliate marketing firms in just four years.

Funding the launch of TrafficBroker with a £2,000 overdraft, he went on to finance his business's outstanding growth with a £160,000 angel investment. By 2006, sales had grown to £18.3m, and by 2008 turnover was expected to hit £25m.

Since then, Hutchinson has picked up the pace, if anything. He has evolved his business, since rebranded as Forward, into a next generation investor with a portfolio of internet businesses. Forward Internet Group buys and transforms businesses such as uSwitch and Factory Media. Forward Labs invents new businesses in-house such as InvisibleHand and Drop Wines. Forward Venture Partners has a portfolio of minority investments in early stage businesses. In 2012, Forward Internet Group was named as one of the UK's fastest growing technology businesses in *The Sunday Times* Tech Track 100, after it acquired one of Europe's largest publishers for biking enthusiasts, as well as being listed in the paper's 100 Best Small Companies to Work For.

Sezer Yurtseven

Company: Pan Energy Markets
Young Gun in: 2010 (Age: 30)
Ex-FTSE trader (and *Big Brother* contestant) Yurtseven had already set up one successful venture by 2010 - Anello FX, a foreign currency brokerage that was handling around £100m a year in currency transactions. His second, Pan Energy Markets, was formed after he identified a gap in the green energy market, and the proprietary trading house, which acted as a financial intermediary bringing buyers and sellers together, saw a turnover of €370m from June 2009 to when he was named a Young Gun in 2010. Despite global expansion, the company went into liquidation in 2012.

Rajesh Agrawal

Company: RationalFX
Young Gun in: 2012 (Age: 34)
With no external funding, Agrawal and co-founder Paresh Davdra have created a business that has grown at a stratospheric rate since its launch in 2005. The foreign exchange company RationalFX has seen the transfer of around $2.7 billion worldwide, has over 25,000 private and business clients, and while margins in the sector are small, turnover stands at a highly impressive £473m. In 2012, Agrawal also launched an online money transfer operation named Xendpay, owned by RationalFX. No surprise, perhaps, that Agrawal scooped the Young Entrepreneur Award at the 36th Asian Who's Who Awards in 2011. The business supported the Marussia F1 Team car at the 2012 Formula 1 Airtel Indian Grand Prix and previously sponsored Birmingham City FC for the 2011-12 season.

Samir Desai, James Meekings and Andrew Mullinger

Company: Funding Circle
Young Gun in: 2012 (Ages: 29)
The concept of sidestepping the banks is an appealing one at present. At Funding Circle, people directly lend their money to small businesses in the UK, supporting the core of the economy in the process. Investors lend from as little as £20 and spread their risk by lending to hundreds of different companies, while businesses gain access to fast finance. The co-founders are hoping that Funding Circle can gain a share of the small business lending market, worth approximately £75 billion. So too are its investors, who include Carphone Warehouse's Sir Charles Dunstone, Betfair founder Ed Wray, Union Square Ventures and Index Ventures. A total of £13.2m has been invested in Funding Circle since the business launched two years ago. The platform has already signed up over 20,000 members, with a total of more than £50m lent to small businesses.

Taavet Hinrikus and Kristo Käärmann

Company: Exchange Solutions/TransferWise
Young Gun in: 2012 (Ages: 30 and 31)
'The Skype of currency exchange' is how TransferWise describes itself, and considering co-founder Hinrikus was Skype's first employee, it's a fairly apt summary. The service allows consumers to send money between UK and European accounts for a fraction of the price banks charge, by using a peer-to-peer crowdsourced model to get the best rate on the exchange. The founders launched in 2010, after becoming fed up with being charged a substantial amount of money when sending money back and forth to their home country of Estonia. Taking on the banks has so far paid off, with the company's exchange volume reaching €10m in its first year. Investors include venture capital firms, as well as the founders of PayPal and Wonga. In early 2013, the business was recognised at The Europas awards as the best European tech company aged under three years, by winning the Best Middleweight Startup award. In doing so it narrowly beat SwiftKey, the mobile keyboard app developed by fellow Young Guns Dr Ben Medlock and Jon Reynolds, which was the runner-up in the same category.

Manufacturing

Jack Glendinning

Company: Its Tiles
Young Gun in: 2003 (Age: 32)
Glendinning was managing farms and forestry estates when in 1994 he saw some electrically heated tiles in South Africa. Instead of starting alone, he joined Mike Curry, who was then running tile company Warmup. After a stuttering start and a long period of R&D, by 2003 its tiles were being sold in Topps Tiles, Tiles-R-Us and independent tile shops, and a variation was available in Focus Wickes and other 'sheds'.

Richard Reed

Company: Innocent Drinks
Young Gun in: 2003 (Age: 30)

Even back in 2003, Innocent Drinks was demonstrating a voracious appetite for publicity. Something about the brand's accessible folksy quirkiness (this was before packaging inevitably carried whimsical messages for consumers) caught the imagination of customers, and founders Richard Reed, Adam Balon and Jon Wright made the most of media and public interest. Even the business's start-up story has now become part of entrepreneurial folklore: in 1999 the three Cambridge University mates set up a stall at a music festival which set out their homemade smoothies alongside a sign asking punters to vote on whether they should quit their day jobs to focus solely on creating fruit smoothies. A resounding 'yes' meant the trio quit their jobs the following day and Innocent Drinks was born.

By the time a 30-year-old Richard Reed was among the first crop of Young Guns four years later, smoothies were on their way to becoming big business. Innocent had overtaken P&J Smoothies as the number one provider of the fruit-based drink, and its turnover had risen from

£400,000 in 1999 to an expected £18m. Expansion to Scandinavia and Benelux was on the cards, and more products were planned.

The co-founders were also determined from the very beginning that theirs would be a business that did things differently. Ethics, sustainability and an anti-corporate ethos were very much part of the image they built around Innocent. The brand's off-beat appeal was characterised by their HQ – a buzzy, artificial turf-floored office they named Fruit Towers – and corporate messaging that was (and still is today) designed to feel witty, personable and happy-go-lucky. Savvy marketing also led the company to start running 'village fetes' and the Fruitstock festival in Regent's Park.

By 2007, Reed was working hard on creating as sustainable a business as possible, while not losing sight of the bottom line. By that time its workforce was 187 strong. Innocent had captured 65% of the domestic market, and a layer of senior management, including a UK managing director, had been woven into the business's close-knit fabric. Turnover had rocketed to £100m. However, Reed had created indelible principles he was integrating throughout the fast-growing company: procuring ethically, reducing and offsetting carbon emissions, recycling and putting something back through charitable giving. Innocent's fruit suppliers had to meet minimum International Labour Organization standards and premium rates were paid to Rainforest Alliance-accredited or local farms. Electricity came from green renewable sources. Fleet vehicles were powered either by biofuels, LPG or hybrid fuels. CO2 emissions were measured each month and offset by 120% to be carbon negative across the business. Innocent was also the first UK company to make its bottles from 50% post-consumer recycled (PCR) plastic; they were to become 100% recycled by 2007.

This may go some way to explaining why Innocent came under such scrutiny, and no shortage of criticism, when in 2009 the founders decided to sell a minority stake of the company to soft drink behemoth (and the most corporate of all corporates) Coca-Cola for £30m. The move was driven by a need to fund expansion into Europe, but Reed found himself having to defend the decision by assuring consumers it wouldn't spell the end of the company's ideals. It marked a challenging moment for the brand, with naysayers even more up in arms in 2010 when Coca-Cola bought a further stake, bringing its ownership to 58%. The disposal of shares by one of the original 'angel' investors in Innocent, as well as a small number of shares sold by the founders, meant that Coca-Cola was now the majority owner, but a legal agreement meant that Reed, Balon and Wright were still able to run the company their way. This meant that initiatives such as the Innocent Foundation, which was set up in 2004 to earmark 10% of profits to 'do good things', remained in place. So far the company has committed £1.3m to good causes.

Today, Innocent is Europe's best-selling smoothie brand and has become a household name (as has Richard Reed - thanks in a large part to appearing in a prime-time slot in the BBC's *Be Your Own Boss*). Forecasting a £200m turnover for 2012, the company employs 250 staff across Europe in offices including Paris, Amsterdam, Hamburg, Salzburg and Copenhagen. It sells over 2 million smoothies each week in 11,000 outlets and has also expanded its product offering significantly, having launched into the food market in 2008 with the 'veg pot', and now selling yoghurts and kids' food as well as juices (launched in 2011) and the This Water brand. In 2011, one in four UK households bought an Innocent product, according to Jon Wright.

European expansion, however, has meant that losses increased by 54% in 2011, according to *The Grocer*, with parent company Fresh Trading recording a pre-tax loss of £9.8m in the year to 31 December 2011, against £6m the year before. However, the company insisted that these were planned losses, as a result of exceptional costs such as growing European subsidiaries and the launch of juices. The same year saw turnover rise 25.4% to £162.7m (£127.5m from the UK), the highest ever revenue for the business.

How and when Reed and the other founders will eventually exit Innocent is a question on which it is interesting to speculate. So far the Coca-Cola investment hasn't been used as an exit strategy and the trio have steered the company with aplomb through difficult times for the brand, not to mention a recession. The naysayers have been proved wrong - and with some style.

Nick Rutter

Company: Sprue Aegis
Young Gun in: 2003 (Age: 31)

It's no exaggeration to say that Sprue Aegis has done its bit in making the world a little safer. At the same time, co-founder Nick Rutter has created a thriving and successful business. University mates Rutter and Sam Tate got talking about business ideas in spring 1998, and by the end of the year Sprue Aegis had been born with a £50,000 grant. The pair decided to design and manufacture a smoke alarm that removed the three key failures of the current models: consumers do not change batteries, they remove batteries after false alarms, and many fail to fit the alarm after buying one. A Sprue Aegis smoke alarm fits into light fittings, uses the main power source and re-sets at the flick of the light switch.

Since then, there has been no stopping the Coventry-based company, which has an expanded range of products that is sold in Tesco and B&Q. Sprue Aegis has also supplied Britain's fire and rescue services. Expansion into international territories is under way as a result of American competitor BRK Brands granting Sprue Aegis the rights to its business in Europe. Turnover for 2011 stood at £33m and the company achieved organic growth of 53% per year from 2008 to 2011. In December 2012, Sprue Aegis and Innocent became the only companies ever to be listed in *The Sunday Times* Fast Track 100 league table for five consecutive years.

Tony Caldeira

Company: Caldeira
Young Gun in: 2004 (Age: 34)
Caldeira created one of the UK's fastest growing companies in a collapsing industry. Started as a market stall in 1991, the St Helens-based cushion manufacturer was turning over £6m by 2004, and employed 130 staff in the UK and a further 100 in China. In the past eight years the textiles company has expanded into the US, opening a store on New York's prestigious Fifth Avenue. Turnover has broken the £20m mark and employee numbers have risen considerably. The business supplies leading retailers in 20 countries. Tony Caldeira himself has unsuccessfully run for Mayor of Liverpool and seen his company feature in two documentaries, *Brits Get Rich in China* on Channel 4 and *The Town Taking on China* on the BBC.

Simon Coyle

Company: Kshocolat
Young Gun in: 2005 (Age: 30)
Coyle was one of the first to realise that the UK chocolate gift market was ripe for modernisation. In 2005, he had established two shops in Scotland and a range of premium products were finding their way onto the shelves of 250 stockists including Waitrose and Liberty. He had also started exporting products to Europe, Japan, Australia and the US. Although the

brand was put into administration in 2010, it was bought by novelty confectioner Bon Bon Buddies.

James Hibbert

Company: Dress2kill
Young Gun in: 2005 (Age: 35)
Hibbert never settles for 'good enough'. Bored in his recruitment job, he quit. Horrified by the lack of enthusiasm shown by a visiting tailor, he launched his own company to do it better. In need of advice, he wrote to and got feedback from Richard Branson and Charles Dunstone. And the market took notice of Dress2kill, too. Offering modern bespoke tailoring starting at £350 through workplaces, online and via partnerships, by 2005 the company had 2,500 customers and 80% repeat business and was on course to double its turnover to £1m.

Zef Eisenberg

Company: Maximuscle
Young Gun in: 2006 (Age: 33)
In 2006, the year that Maximuscle founder Zef Eisenberg was named a Young Gun, he pointed out to *Growing Business* magazine that his company was operating in 'the most challenging and regulated industry around'. The degree to which this entirely failed to hold him back is evidenced in his eventual, lucrative exit from his business: Maximuscle was sold to GlaxoSmithKlein in 2010 for a staggering £162m.

Maximuscle was 10 years old in 2006, and sector domination was very much under way. The training and nutrition education service, based in Watford, had signed up high-profile clients including the England cricket team and the RFU; turnover had reached £21m and market share stood at 43%. Perhaps more importantly, the market itself was still a relatively immature one, one which Maximuscle was single-handedly galvanising.

This pioneering firm came into being as a result of Eisenberg's experience in body building. In 1993, he shook the market after writing and publishing an exposé on which products would help build muscle and burn fat and which were a waste of money. From the following this gained, and profits from the book's first print run, he started a business offering the products he trusted. He also began providing extensive educational tools. Before long, the company formed a partnership with key manufacturers to create own-brand products. 'It was unique in the industry at the time and led to the creation of the brand. The products were not formulated on price, but on quality and scientific research,' he told *Growing Business*.

Maximuscle products built up a loyal following among elite athletes in particular, but the company faced a tough time after a media storm broke over some athletes blaming sport nutrition products for positive results in drugs tests. Eisenberg knew the facts were on his side, however. Every batch of Maximuscle products was independently drug-screened, and the company was spending around £200,000 each year putting all of its products through a stringent WADA (World Anti-Doping Agency)-approved drugs screening lab.

Eisenberg launched an energetic defence of his products, exploiting the inevitable press interest, and in doing so turned a near-disaster for the company into invaluable positive PR as the firm secured hundreds of column inches.

The firm continued to grow, and until 2003 had done so without taking on any debt or giving away any equity. But, driven by a desire to attract high-calibre talent to his management team, Eisenberg started to think about a management buyout. To this effect, a buy-in chairman joined from Lee Cooper, where he was chief executive, and a buy-in managing director came from a position as group marketing director at Premier Foods. A private equity backer was found in Piper Private Equity in a deal valued at £10m and finalised in 2004.

As a result of this, 'I realised the business needed to take a gentle shift in a different direction,' Eisenberg told *Growing Business*, namely in terms

> **I realised the business needed to take a gentle shift in a different direction.**

of making the brand more appealing among mainstream consumers, as well as with professional athletes. This focus was very effective, helped by a marketing strategy focused on endorsements from top athletes;

'ambassadors' have included rugby union international Ugo Monye, long jumper Greg Rutherford and boxer Amir Khan. Maximuscle continued to increase market share and launch new products and, in 2007, Darwin Private Equity bought a majority stake in the business for £75m.

Three years later, GlaxoSmithKlein bought Maximuscle. As Eisenberg told *Growing Business*: 'With private equity an exit after three or four years is always likely.' A trade sale wasn't necessarily part of the plan, but the £162m offered was in the end 'a price we couldn't refuse', Eisenberg said. The largest single shareholder after the Darwin deal, he made a full exit as soon as the firm became part of GSK.

Since then, Eisenberg has been focusing on growing his investment portfolio and in 2011 launched a £150m fund to invest in health and fitness businesses. The smart money says we'll be hearing more from this dynamic entrepreneur.

Haani Ul Hasnain

Company: Haani Cables
Young Gun in: 2007 (Age: 29)
Rocket scientist to entrepreneur isn't a leap many tend to make. But this didn't put off aerospace engineering graduate Haani Ul Hasnain. Following a change in career plans, Hasnain joined his father's cable manufacturing firm after leaving university, and spent six years working his way up while honing his leadership skills studying part time for an MBA. By the time he was in his third year as CEO, he had reinvented the company, streamlined processes, reinvested £3.5m, doubled turnover and grown it from 40 to 130 staff. Today he focuses on providing guidance and support for others hoping to unlock their potential.

Matthew Stevenson

Company: Reef One
Young Gun in: 2007 (Age: 31)
Product design and marketing graduate Matthew Stevenson set up Reef One with his father in 1999 after creating an ultra-stylish fishbowl with a unique filtration system. The company developed a flagship product, the biOrb, alongside a number of new offerings, many of which are world firsts. Completely self-funded, the firm had achieved a £4.5m turnover in

2007, had sales offices in Paris and LA, and sold its products through distributors in 15 countries. The company has sold over a million biOrbs so far.

Priya Lakhani

Company: Masala Masala
Young Gun in: 2009 (Age: 28)
Former libel lawyer Priya Lakhani gave up a promising law career to launch her Indian cooking sauces, which use only fresh, authentic ingredients to make a supermarket range that she proudly claims tastes 'as good as [her] mother's'. Masala Masala's sauces were being stocked by major retailers Waitrose, Ocado, Harvey Nichols, Harrods and Budgens, only a year after launch. Lakhani has proved that even start-ups can afford hefty corporate social responsibility strategies - an underprivileged person in India is given a hot meal for every pot of Masala Masala sold.

Graham Bosher

Company: Graze
Young Gun in: 2009 (Age: 27)
Graham Bosher, one of the founders of successful movie rental business LOVEFiLM, is living proof that adapting an existing business model can prove to be as good as inventing a new one. Rather than sending out movies by post, Graze, which was established by Bosher in 2009, offers a service that delivers healthy snacks. Turnover in 2007 was an impressive £2.5m, and the company had just received a £2m investment from Octopus Ventures and DFJ Esprit. Today the business has sales of around £20m and delivers its snack boxes to more than 100,000 UK customers. At the end of 2012 the business went through a management buyout backed by the Carlyle Group. As part of the deal, CEO Bosher successfully exited, and has taken on a non-executive director role. Bosher also saw LOVEFiLM sold to Amazon for £200m in 2011.

Imran Hakim

Company: iTeddy
Young Gun in: 2009 (Age: 31)
After successfully securing a £140,000 investment from Peter Jones and Theo Paphitis during his assured appearance on the BBC's *Dragons' Den*, Bolton-based entrepreneur Imran Hakim saw demand explode for iTeddy, the product he developed. Essentially, the innovative combination of a cuddly bear and a media player, iTeddy performed impressively in UK stores. This resulted in the award of a global distribution deal with Britain's largest independent toy company, Vivid Imaginations, at the end of 2007. Meanwhile, Hakim, who has won countless business and industry awards, also owns a variety of other companies, including a chain of optometrists in the north-west. Today he concentrates on incubating and investing in other companies.

Fraser Doherty

Company: SuperJam
Young Gun in: 2009 (Age: 20)
Fraser Doherty's SuperJam was founded when, aged just 14 years old, he spotted the untapped potential of his gran's jam recipes. After successful trials at farmers' markets, he became the youngest stockist to a major supermarket when he signed a deal to supply Waitrose in 2007. Today, Doherty sells his 100% fruit jam in more than 2,000 stores (including Waitrose, Sainsbury's, Morrisons and Asda) across eight different countries, including Germany and Australia, and the young entrepreneur plans to expand to the USA. In 2012, Doherty launched SuperHoney, an initiative to set up beehives in schools and community areas and sell the produce in leading supermarkets.

Simon Duffy and Rhodri Ferrier

Company: Bulldog Natural Grooming
Young Gun in: 2009 (Ages: 32 and 30)
Simon Duffy and Rhodri Ferrier raised £1.2m in angel investment to launch Bulldog in 2007, and in doing so created a market for natural and ethically sourced male grooming products. The range, which Duffy and

Ferrier proudly proclaim has been created for men, by men, rather than being 'your girlfriend's brand rebadged', proved to be highly popular. The products can now be found in major retail outlets throughout the UK, and Duffy and Ferrier are seeing them win international fans, being sold in the US, Australia, Germany, Norway, New Zealand, Sweden, Japan, Ireland and South Korea.

Warren Bennett and David Hathiramani

Company: A Suit That Fits
Young Gun in: 2009 (Ages: 28)
Started as an online tailor, A Suit That Fits owned three permanent stores by 2009, boasting 40 billion design combinations and a turnover above £2.4m. Today the world's first online tailoring company has expanded to 33 stores UK-wide, employing over 50 staff. Now turning over £3m annually, the business's awards include the Barclays Customer Focus Award (SME) at the UK Customer Service Awards 2012 and Smaller Etailer, Drapers Fashion Awards 2011.

James Watt and Martin Dickie

Company: BrewDog
Young Gun in: 2009 (Ages: 26)
Bored of the industrially brewed lagers and stuffy ales that dominate the UK beer market, BrewDog founders James Watt and Martin Dickie, at the age of only 24, decided to brew their own 'classic beers with a contemporary twist'. The firm is now Scotland's largest independent brewery, and its brands are listed in Tesco, Asda, Sainsbury's and Oddbins, as well as being available in numerous countries outside the UK. Watt and Dickie chose a modern and innovative way to fund BrewDog's growth, and completed two funding rounds which, through the BrewDog website, offered people the opportunity to buy shares in the company. As a result there are now more than 7,000 shareholders, and the business has raised over £2.2m. BrewDog today has bars in Aberdeen (where it recently opened a new production facility to keep up with demand), Edinburgh, Glasgow and Camden and has been recognised as one of the UK's fastest growing companies, ranking at number 29 in the 2012 *Sunday Times* Fast Track 100 league.

Anthony Lau

Company: Cyclehoop
Young Gun in: 2010 (Age: 29)
Lau's business, started in 2008, is based on the Cyclehoop, a simple yet groundbreaking bike stand. By 2010, when Lau was named a Young Gun, it had already found favour with Transport for London (TfL) and councils across the UK. Today the company is producing over 15 products and selling them in 10 different countries, including Germany, Luxembourg, Finland and the USA. Contracted by TfL, Cyclehoop provided 6,000 bicycle spaces for use during the Olympic Games, acting as the sole bike parking provider for the event. Following a lucrative new deal in Vancouver, turnover was expected to reach £1.3m in 2012.

Damon Bonser

Company: Spinning Hat
Young Gun in: 2010 (Age: 32)
London-based creative design and manufacturing company Spinning Hat specialises in creating original fun gifts for 16 to 35-year-olds. It's an offer that has attracted an impressive array of high-profile clients to date, including John Lewis, Urban Outfitters, The Conran Shop and Barnes & Noble. Damon Bonser set up the business in 2005, with the launch of the world's first counting bottle opener – the Bottle Spy.

Adam King and Jake Allen

Company: King & Allen
Young Gun in: 2010 (Ages: 33 and 31)
King & Allen, formed in 2003, makes suits that follow the same tailoring guidelines and use similar cloth as those made on Savile Row, but that cost a fraction of the price. The firm hires function rooms across the UK and turns them into a tailor's shop for the day. Meanwhile, its 'low-key' tailoring centres carry no stock, thereby keeping overheads low. In a highly competitive market, King & Allen is carving itself a profitable niche, and the founders now claim theirs to be the UK's most popular bespoke tailoring company.

Hayley Gait-Golding

Company: BEAR
Young Gun in: 2010 (Age: 30)
As a personal trainer, BEAR founder Hayley Gait-Golding was frequently confronted by people struggling to find healthy but tasty treats. From this BEAR was born, with the added benefits of being reasonably priced and with attractive, fun branding. Launched in 2009, BEAR turned over a respectable £2.2m in its first year. Gait-Golding's goal is to supply the nation's favourite snack, and the bags of fruit or grain are proving popular with health-conscious office workers. Stockists include Waitrose, Asda, Harrods, Co-op, Somerfield, Holland & Barrett and Sainsbury's.

Julie Diem Le

Company: Zoobug
Young Gun in: 2010 (Age: 33)
Former eye surgeon Julie Diem Le has seen her business achieve global distribution and by 2010 was making good progress in travel retail as well as in the optical sector, with her glasses stocked in duty-free shops in international airports. Today the Zoobug collections are distributed in more than 21 countries worldwide, and are available in leading opticians and department stores including Harrods and Selfridges.

Ning Li, Chloe Macintosh and Julien Callède

Company: Made.com
Young Gun in: 2010 (Ages: 30, 37 and 29)
Launched on a £2.5m investment, the made-to-order furniture site took off rapidly, and today delivers more than 100,000 items per year, turning over in excess of £2m in the process. The company raised £7m in early 2012, currently employs 80 people across two offices in London and Shanghai, and has extended its manufacturing network to five different countries. In September 2012, the online furniture site launched a physical showroom, complete with QR codes and miniature 3D-printed models of the furniture.

Dr Shamus Husheer and Dr Oriane Chausiaux

Company: Cambridge Temperature Concepts (trading as DuoFertility)
Young Gun in: 2012 (Ages: 35 and 31)
Options for couples struggling to conceive can appear limited. The founders of DuoFertility believe their product can help couples conceive naturally, to avoid resorting to invasive procedures. A small patch is placed under the woman's arm and establishes when she is at her most fertile. The information can be uploaded via the internet and analysed by a team of fertility experts; they then provide the support to the woman, in the comfort of her own home, that is normally associated with a high-end fertility clinic. Cambridge Temperature Concepts was founded in 2006 and won multiple awards and business plan competitions. It is now funded by the Cambridge Angels, Cambridge Capital Group, Downing Enterprise and private investors. The East of England Development Agency has also provided several development grants to the company. The DuoFertility product costs £500 but the business has a money-back guarantee if pregnancy doesn't occur within 12 months. The company employs around 30 staff, and its product is just starting to be sold in the USA, which represents a huge market, one where it has already received endorsement from medics. In the UK, its stockists include Boots, and it is being used in a pilot by the NHS.

Richard Baister

Company: SUMO Drinks
Young Gun in: 2012 (Age: 30)
By using natural ingredients that raise the body's metabolic rate for up to three hours after consumption, Richard Baister's soft drinks are billed as 'the refreshing way to burn calories'. SUMO Drinks launched in 2011 after a three-year development process, and they are already being stocked in over 850 stores. Baister is becoming something of an expert in soft drinks start-ups, having founded the world's first range of flavoured energy drinks - Velocity - in 2005. He sold the brand in 2008 to concentrate on SUMO Drinks, and, with funding from the European Investment Bank, as well as some major international distribution contracts, the decision is looking like a wise one so far.

Mobile technologies

Christina Domecq

Company: SpinVox
Young Gun in: 2006 (Age: 29)
Spanish-born Domecq exploited a simple idea - turning voicemails into texts. By 2006 SpinVox had 120,000 users, with six languages available, and had raised £25m in investments. The money kept coming and the start-up raised a total of $230m. However, this couldn't prevent fractures forming and, despite having built a reputation as a star of the UK tech scene, the company was eventually sold to Nuance, an American rival, for just $102m.

David Springall

Company: YoSpace
Young Gun in: 2006 (Age: 32)
Founded in 1999 with Tim Sewell, the long-awaited uptake of 3G mobiles and consumer-generated content saw YoSpace finally deliver on its promise by 2006. Delivering content for the likes of Vodafone, Orange, 3 and Emap - as well as its own products such as LookAtMe! - an impressive 100% growth was predicted for 2007. No surprise, perhaps, that an acquisition was on the cards, and in February 2007 the company was bought by Emap for £8.7m. Subsequently, Emap itself was acquired by H. Bauer Publishing. In March 2009, Bauer Media sold its interest in YoSpace to private investors, and the company now operates as an independently owned business. David Springall has remained with his company as chief technology officer throughout its changes in ownership.

Jeremy Bygrave

Company: Mediaburst
Young Gun in: 2006 (Age: 32)
A difficult year resulted in an impressive re-alignment by serial entrepreneur Bygrave. As a result of regulatory changes, Mediaburst was forced to focus solely on business messaging, rather than on the premium-rate competitions that had provided 80% of revenues. He also set about streamlining and refocusing, thereby keeping Mediaburst afloat and increasing margins. He remained with the company only until 2008, however, and now heads up marketing company 8 Ball Games, which specialises in running its own online gaming sites and whose main brand is loveyourbingo.com.

Barry Houlihan

Company: Mobile Interactive Group
Young Gun in: 2006 (Age: 34)
Houlihan's Mobile Interactive Group (MIG) was only two years old in 2006 yet made £21m that year. Founded from a division of O2, Houlihan put his company's success down to the core staff he took with him and the speed with which they develop mobile-based technology. He admitted that pacing the company's growth was like 'holding onto a wild horse'. MIG's fast-rising trajectory saw it scoop top ranking in both *The Sunday Times* Tech Track 100 in 2008 and the 2010 Deloitte Technology Fast 500 EMEA. In 2011, with 160 employees, a £100m plus turnover, and clients such as PepsiCo, Skype, Sony and Vodafone, American corporation Velti acquired the company for $59m.

Alastair Lukies

Company: Monitise
Young Gun in: 2007 (Age: 33)

It's typical that the bigger a company gets, the slower its growth. This has not been the case with Monitise, which enables customers to use mobile phones to access their bank accounts.

The company was small but rapidly expanding when its founder was named a 2007 Young Gun, and today – a big beast in the world of UK tech start-ups – it is the third fastest growing technology company in the UK.

What Monitise has done is nothing short of staggering. Not only is it the leader in its field, it's a field that didn't really exist until it came along. Smartphones are completely transforming the way we pay, shop and bank, and Alastair Lukies and co-founder Steve Atkinson (previously of Vodafone) were two of the first to spot what was going to happen. Thanks to their prescience, Monitise has been able to be at the front of the pack since day one. Of course, being ahead of the game means you are placed in the position of having to educate in order to sell. It was initially a challenge persuading financial institutions and mobile networks of the merits of a single platform users could access no matter who they banked with. But it was a challenge they've overcome and then some: partners of Monitise's Mobile Money offering now total over 300, including most major banks and mobile operators.

Monitise's stomach-lurchingly quick ascent effectively began in 2007, when it spun out of London Stock Exchange-listed tech giant Morse and floated on AIM. It raised £21.4m, and in 2008 won the AIM New Business of the Year award at the Fast Growth Business Awards, with the judges singling out the company's potential to 'transform an industry' in particular. Although the impact of the credit crunch was felt quickly, a five-year exclusive contract with VISA in 2009 (which also bought a 14% stake in the company) put it on an even keel. The company has recorded a staggering growth rate of 2,875% since floating, as a result of which Monitise was ranked number three in the Deloitte Technology Fast 50, the renowned awards programme that charts the UK's fastest growing tech companies. In 2011, it was twelfth in the list. The company's revenues are expected to hit at least £70m in the 2013 financial year, up from £36.1m in 2011, which in turn had grown from just £15.3m in 2010. As Lukies said recently: 'Our business is seeing enormous demand for Mobile Money services. The breadth of companies interested in working with us has never been greater and the level of consumer engagement with Mobile Money services we have developed is hitting new highs.'

Much of this growth has been driven by Monitise's global reach. It has expanded internationally through joint ventures and licensing deals, and has live services in the UK, the US, India and Africa. It has recently dramatically increased its presence in the US - expected to be the world's largest market in mobile payments and banking - by acquiring its biggest rival. US firm ClairMail was itself seeing year-on-year revenue growth of 90% and turning over £11m when it was acquired for £90m in 2012, and its impact on Monitise has been to further solidify its position as the leader in mobile money globally. It's no surprise Lukies has his sights set over the pond when it's taken into consideration that 111 million US consumers are expected to be using mobile banking by 2016, while mobile commerce revenues are forecast to hit £31 billion by the same year.

The growth potential of mobile money, particularly via mobile commerce, is only just now starting to be realised.

Perhaps then it is only to be expected that, despite the value of payments and transfers handled by the company growing from $1 billion a year ago to more than $25 billion today, Monitise is still seen by many as a mere minnow when compared with how big it could potentially become. Lukies has definitely got his eye firmly set on the future. To this end, in 2012 he announced plans to look to the markets in order to raise £100m, which will be the company's seventh, and largest, round of fundraising. He says: 'The growth potential of mobile money, particularly via mobile commerce, is only just now starting to be realised. Proceeds from our proposed capital raising will be used to rapidly scale our business and enhance our mobile commerce capabilities.'

He has also indicated that the company has outgrown AIM, and will be looking to move to the London Stock Exchange in 2013, despite speculation over a move to the NASDAQ.

Despite Monitise's all-conquering outlook, the company is yet to become profitable. However, looking to the long term, this is a company that is as well placed as any to become one of Britain's most successful ever technology firms. As Lukies says: 'The future of payments, the internet, retail and social networking is all mobile.' A mobile future is a bright one for Monitise.

Alistair Crane

Company: Grapple Mobile
Young Gun in: 2012 (Age: 26)
Alistair Crane's career working with brands started at a mere 16 years of age in the advertising and sales division of Northern & Shell, publishers of *OK!* magazine and the *Daily Express*. By the age of 26, Crane had become a respected figure within the mobile industry and he had built up an impressive client roster. McDonald's, P&G and Adidas are among the 90 plus brands for which his company, Grapple, has developed mobile applications. Co-founding Grapple at 23 years of age, in just two years Crane had grown the company from 5 to 85 staff globally, and it claims to be Europe's most awarded mobile agency. Inclusions within the highly coveted NMA Top 100 and The Drum Digital 100 'Ones to Watch' have established Grapple as the digital agency to keep an eye on in the future. The business has enjoyed year-on-year growth since inception, which is particularly impressive considering that Grapple was founded in a double-dip recession and has received no venture capital funding.

Jude Ower

Company: PlayMob
Young Gun in: 2012 (Age: 31)
Jude Ower is an old hand when it comes to gaming, specifically gaming for educational purposes. She has been developing educational games for over a decade, and is a major player in this field. PlayMob, which she founded in 2007, explores the potential for charities to raise money through games. It has created a platform that allows game players to buy in-game objects, for example a tree or building, with the profits going to charity. In this way, Ower believes, charities can connect with people who

may not normally give. In total, the business has raised around $1m in investment from business angels, Nesta, Midven and investors such as Bill Liao (co-founder of Xing), Sarah du Heaume (founder of Just Media) and PlayMob's chairman, Ian Livingstone, to name but a few.

Dr Ben Medlock and Jon Reynolds

Company: SwiftKey (trading as Touch Type)
Young Gun in: 2012 (Ages: 32 and 26)
SwiftKey is causing something of a buzz in the UK tech start-up scene, and it's easy to see why. By combing through SMS, email, etc., the app takes note of the user's commonly used phrases and, using natural language technology, much more accurately predicts the next word and corrects spelling mistakes. It was downloaded 50,000 times on the day it was launched in 2010, and by the time the entrepreneurs were 2012 Young Guns, it had been downloaded over 15 million times. In fact, in 2012 it was the best-selling Android app. Revenue has so far been generated through sales of the app, but another significant stream has been added through licensing the software. The two Cambridge graduates have won three leading industry awards already and have raised £2.5m in external funding.

Ben Whitaker, Tom Godber and Ed Howson

Company: Masabi
Young Gun in: 2012 (Ages: 34)
Queues, always unwelcome, are even more frustrating when you are running late for a train and need to buy a ticket. Masabi could signal the end of ticket queues with its 'ticket machine in your pocket' app. As the leading developer of mobile ticketing technology, it allows passengers to buy and display tickets on most mobile phones - not just smartphones. Founded in 2002, the company works in partnership with firms such as thetrainline.com and is deployed with operators including Virgin Trains, Chiltern Railways, First Capital Connect and many more. Backed by venture firm m8 Capital to the tune of $6m over two rounds, the company is racking up industry awards, and in 2012 started to work within the USA with transit agencies such as MBTA Boston and MTA New York.

Jay Bregman

Company: Hailo
Young Gun in: 2012 (Age: 33)
Hailo is using the ubiquity of smartphones in order to help out anyone who's spent too long trying to find a cab (so, all of us), as well as cabbies themselves. Its black cab app allows users to hail, virtually, a licensed taxi in just a couple of taps on their phone. Cab drivers use the app to ensure that they get the highest possible number of jobs in a shift. The app also works for drivers as a social network, allowing them to share information with each other (on traffic, say). By January 2012, the app had been downloaded 150,000 times. The company represents Bregman's second bite of the cherry - the first start-up he was involved with was the incredibly successful eCourier - and so far he has raised around $20m from investors.

Online business services

Dr Aydin Kurt-Elli

Company: Lumison
Young Gun in: 2004 (Age: 30)
Edinburgh-based Lumison, formerly edNET, was founded by Kurt-Elli almost 10 years ago. However, he left the business in order to work as a junior doctor, returning in 1999 and then resurrecting its fortunes. The IT firm had reached a turnover of £3m by 2004, and, since then, growth has continued steadily. After interest from potential buyers, Dr Kurt-Elli sold a majority stake to a private equity firm in 2010. The business has since been rebranded as Pulsant, and Dr Kurt-Elli remains as chief operating officer.

Matt McNeill

Companies: Sign-up.to, eTickets.to
Young Gun in: 2007 (Age: 26)
McNeill was designing music websites while studying for A-levels, and, despite gaining a place at Oxford, he deferred to focus on business pursuits. His second venture, Sign-up.to, allows businesses to manage their own email and mobile marketing campaigns. Sister company eTickets.to allows consumers to buy tickets direct from event promoters. Sign-up.to remains privately owned and has staff working in Woking and Brisbane, Australia.

Shaa Wasmund

Companies: Brightstation Ventures, Osoyou, Miomi
Young Gun in: 2007 (Age: 35)
Serial entrepreneur Wasmund turned down the position of CEO at Bebo (and the sizeable equity stake that went with it) after falling in 'the business equivalent of love at first sight' with business partner Dan Wagner. In 2007, they managed the $100m Brightstation Ventures fund, had a 50%

stake in Shiny Media (along with fellow Young Gun Ben Way), and had worked on a number of new ventures, including timeline history site Miomi. Today Wasmund's primary focus is business advice site smarta.com, which she launched in 2009.

Richard Moross

Company: Moo
Young Gun in: 2008 (Age: 30)
Soon after launching Moo in 2004, Richard Moross began to realise the growing potential of Web 2.0 sites. Since then, relationships with the likes of Facebook and photo-sharing site Flickr have allowed customers to grab their photos and put them on stationery products, including business cards and greetings cards, which are printed and shipped all over the world. The company is now one of the world's fastest growing online printers, has a staff of over 60, and has raised over $5m in venture capital from The Accelerator Group, Index Ventures and Atlas Ventures. In September 2012, Moo bought web-building company Flavors.me from HiiDef Inc. as part of a strategy to expand its digital capabilities. 'We don't currently have acquisition targets in mind,' Moross told *Growing Business*, 'but as with the somewhat opportunistic acquisition of Flavors, we're always interested in strategically aligned investments that will help us realise our vision faster or more comprehensively.'

Adam Hildreth

Company: Crisp Thinking
Young Gun in: 2008 (Age: 23)
Having set up teen website Dubit at 14, Hildreth had already almost a decade of online experience under his belt by 2008, as well as an estimated personal fortune of £25m. Crisp Thinking was launched to provide online child protection technology to clients including service providers, children's virtual worlds and social networks. Crisp Thinking's technology roots out online predators by analysing conversation patterns, typing speed, use of grammar and punctuation. It looks at hundreds of factors on a software 'fingerprint' that can ascertain whether a user is grooming a young person online. The company today describes itself as a global leader in community management software. The Crisp SaaS platform

manages all kinds of online communities including forums, social media channels and online games. It analyses conversations to understand what is being said, in order to help companies moderate their sites while gaining an insight into the community using them. Today, the multimillion-pound business manages some of the world's largest communities for over 100 global brands. It has received investment of approximately $9m.

Matt Hagger

Companies: e-Man, Bizk.it, Zkatter
Young Gun in: 2009 (Age: 30)
Matt Hagger is a compulsive entrepreneur. In 2001, he created Net Sorcerer, an application for real-time news updates that earned him a patent and £100,000 of government funding. The concept was used to develop Sky Sports Alerts. Having co-founded award-winning digital agency e-Man at 21, Hagger has consulted on desktop technology for Warner Music, and raised €1m for Bizk.it, an enterprise application supported by Adobe and Sun Microsystems. He also launched Zkatter, a platform for live mobile video broadcasting, which he says is the most exciting project he's worked on.

Andy McLoughlin and Alastair Mitchell

Company: Huddle
Young Gun in: 2009 (Ages: 30 and 32)
Launched in 2007, Huddle provides online collaboration tools for business. Within two years the firm had raised $5m in venture funding from Eden Ventures and was employing 20 staff. Huddle has experienced explosive international growth since 2009 and is currently used by more than 80% of UK central government and over 100,000 organisations globally. The company has raised more than $40m in venture funding from top-tier US venture capital firms Matrix Partners, Jafco, DAG Ventures and In-Q-Tel (the venture arm of the CIA) and now employs more than 150 people across London, San Francisco and New York.

Alicia Navarro

Company: Skimlinks
Young Gun in: 2010 (Age: 35)
Alicia Navarro launched her business in 2008 in Australia, before heading to Europe, adapating the model and starting to crack the London market. As one of a small number of female technology entrepreneurs in the UK, she immersed herself in the world of technology start-ups before forming Skimlinks as a stand-alone platform to help other businesses monetise their editorial content. By 2010 Skimlinks had 20 employees and £35m worth of transactions going through the platform every year and had raised £1.6m. The company, which aggregates and automates the process of creating affiliate links, now has 50 employees based in both London and San Francisco. With funding totalling £5m, Skimlinks is now a comprehensive content monetisation platform, helping blogs, forums, content networks, newspapers, apps and start-ups monetise their content.

Antony Chesworth

Company: EKM Systems
Young Gun in: 2010 (Age: 30)
One in every five online shops is powered by ekmPowershop, the system Antony Chesworth developed in his bedroom. In the early struggle to get customers, he racked up £25,000 of debt, but perseverance meant that by 2010 he was seeing 500 new clients every month. In 2012 the company acquired leading competitor Tiger Commerce and began expanding into foreign markets. EKM Systems has worked with over 30,000 clients and operates in several countries across the globe.

Damian Kimmelman

Company: Duedil
Young Gun in: 2011 (Age 29)
Founded in 2011, Duedil now stands proudly as the largest database of free company financial information in the world. Its name is short for 'due diligence', the process of researching a company prior to a business deal, and everything about its offering is designed to help busy executives make informed decisions on mergers, acquisitions and investments.

Duedil aggregates information on millions of businesses, from all manner of sources, covering everything from key financials to directors' biographies and health and safety records. The business has now also made Companies House documents available to download. Its user base already spans the globe and encompasses all points on the business spectrum, from sole traders to multinationals.

David Excell

Company: Featurespace
Young Gun in: 2011 (Age: 30)
Cambridge University spin-off Featurespace is seriously smart, specialising in predictive behavioural modelling software serving, primarily, online businesses. Essentially, the company's products help clients understand their online customers, and predict their value and future behaviour.

Founded in 2005, the company impressed angel investors, along with Nesta, to the tune of a seven-figure investment round in which some investors had to be turned away. In 2012, a £1.5m funding round was led by Imperial Innovations Group and also included existing investors Nesta, Cambridge Angels and Cambridge Capital Group, as well as Mike Lynch, non-executive director of Featurespace and founder and ex-CEO of Autonomy.

Co-founder David Excell believes that: 'Featurespace will become the industry standard for consumer businesses, enabling them to understand their individual customers through our unique self-learning algorithms.' Today it already dominates the online betting and gambling market (with customers including Betfair) and the plan now is to expand into other markets, including financial services and e-commerce, and to continue its focus on new product innovations.

Rob Durkin

Company: FusePump
Young Gun in: 2011 (Age: 25)
Just two years after its foundation, by 2011 the online marketing specialist FusePump was on target to achieve a £2m turnover; a plethora of big names, including John Lewis, Waitrose, Sky and Thomas Cook, had already signed up to its leading-edge service, which offers data feeds to market customers' products through many online channels. Although the company

was formed in the middle of the economic downturn, when many potential customers were scaling back on marketing spend, growth has remained consistent and untroubled almost from day one.

Founder Rob Durkin says his company is thriving because British companies are 'very keen to adopt new marketing techniques and strategies'. However, the business is also gaining considerable traction in America, and further overseas expansion is likely in the near future.

Ross Williams

Company: Global Personals
Young Gun in: 2011 (Age: 33)
No one has benefited from the online dating explosion more than Ross Williams. It is only nine years since he set up his own web-based dating service, Global Personals, and it is now firmly entrenched as Europe's largest privately owned dating company. In 2012, revenues hit £46m. The company operates a portfolio of more than 7,500 sites and works with more than 1,500 brand name partners around the world. Match.com is its nearest competitor, and its revenues, Williams says with a trace of well justified satisfaction, are 50% lower than those of Global Personals. In 2012 – for the third year running – the company was named in *The Sunday Times* Fast Track league as one of the UK's fastest growing companies. And Williams remains by far the largest single shareholder, owning 72.5% of the company.

One of the drivers of the business's success, says Williams, is the fact that while online dating is growing, the area with most potential is that of niche sites. People are looking for quality over quantity when they start the online search for Mr or Mrs Right, and Global Personals' sites are based on meeting people of a similar age, interests, ethnicity, and so on. The vast majority of the business's revenues come from its WhiteLabelDating.com platform, which enables brands (such as the *Independent* and GMG Radio) and individuals to power their own dating sites. It provides the dating software, membership database, payment processing, customer support, hosting infrastructure and much more. This means that Global Personals' portfolio is crammed full of successful, often niche, sites. In August 2012 alone, over 775,000 members joined a dating site powered by WhiteLabel-Dating.com, and, amazingly, 98% of the UK's dating sites are now powered by Global Personals.

This means, however, that if the Windsor-based company is to keep growing at its current rate, it must look beyond the UK. The scale of Global Personals' potential becomes clearer in the context of expansion into the US. 'No one does WhiteLabel over there,' says Williams. 'There are no real niche dating companies. And the thing about our business model that gives us an advantage is that we work on a partnership basis, essentially a franchise basis, which means our partners incur the marketing costs. And for an online dating company, that's by far and away the biggest cost. The costs of infrastructure and so on are marginal, whereas acquisition is very costly.'

The US represents a $1.2 billion market. In the UK, the company has conquered between 35% and 40% of the market, so simple maths tells us that it's worth the company investing in a few transatlantic flights. 'The other opportunity we have,' says Williams, 'is that we can sell members other sites. So in the US, Match.com might sell you eHarmony, but that's about it. We can offer you lots of other sites based on your profile.'

To this end, 2013 will be the year in which Global Personals focuses on solidifying its US operation and Williams is thinking of relocating himself for the project. An office, not staffed, has also been established in Australia, though primarily for the purpose of establishing media partnerships.

Like all those running digital businesses, Williams has had to ensure that Global Personals is keeping up to date with how people are accessing websites. It launched its mobile interface in summer 2012, and already 30–40% of its traffic comes via mobile, as does one in four of its daily acquisitions. Williams expects half of its traffic to be coming through mobile within 12 months. It's more difficult to monetise, he admits, but he is staying ahead of the curve and rolling out on iOS, Android and Tablet in 2013. 'We're innovating with the launch of the iPhone 5, for example; we're planning well ahead of the game.' What this means is including features such as being able to upload photos on mobile. It may sound like a small thing, says Williams, 'but that matters, because people message more if there are photos. And more messages mean more revenue.'

Being privately owned means none of the revenue is siphoned off to external shareholders. In the beginning, Williams and his business partner funded the initial overheads by putting debt on credit cards. 'We had half a dozen each,' he says, 'and paid for all the advertising on them, moving the balance and juggling them until the money started coming in.' Today the company isn't short of potential investors, but with the company growing at its present rate, there is little incentive to pursue the offers.

> **We had half a dozen credit cards each and paid for all the advertising on them . . . juggling them until the money started coming in.**

Even acquisitions have been carried out without the need for fundraising. In 2012, Global Personals acquired Smooch.com, a strategic acquisition that provided the firm with access to the freemium model. There are a lot of people who use dating sites for free, and although the paid-for space is much more valuable, and Williams is primarily focused on subscriptions, there are still opportunities to produce revenue in the freemium space. People will pay smaller amounts for restricted content, pictures for example, and their information also allows advertisers to target effectively.

Global Personals describes itself on its website as having 'the heart of a start-up in the body of a grown-up'. But while Global Personals is not exactly small fry in the UK, Williams explains that 'in terms of international businesses, we are still a start-up, so now we're looking at how to grow and scale internationally'. Having thoroughly consolidated the UK online dating market, it's no stretch to imagine Global Personals replicating their success in other territories. They're not household names, but Global Personals – and Ross Williams – are ones to remember.

Duane Jackson

Company: KashFlow
Young Gun in: 2011 (Age: 32)
The world of accountancy software is one dominated by a few very large players. Signs are, though, that this is about to change, with hungry, nimble and responsive start-ups springing up to give small businesses in particular alternative ways of managing their accounts. Duane Jackson's KashFlow is one of the best examples, as borne out by its multiple victories in the annual Business Software Satisfaction Awards. The company was founded in 2006 as one of the first to use the software-as-a-service business model, and secured early investment from Lord Young, the former government minister and successful entrepreneur. Jackson doesn't have a typical entrepreneurial or IT background, with his journey to successful managing director including a spell at Her Majesty's pleasure, but

KashFlow already had over 10,000 customers in 2011, and this is one entrepreneur who seems destined for big things.

Simon Best

Company: BaseKit
Young Gun in: 2011 (Age: 32)
BaseKit is going places. It's not just us that think so – the DIY web-build business closed an investment round worth around $11m in 2011, and won the annual competition at technology start-up incubator Seedcamp. Furthermore, by the time founder Simon Best was named a 2011 Young Gun, it already had around 2,000 paying subscribers, and the company is targeting a 30–40% profit margin, on a $100m turnover, within four years.

Best co-founded BaseKit with brother Richard and friend Richard Healy – all experienced web developers – in 2009, and the business is his second start-up. In 2011 the company rolled out in Latin America and further international openings are imminent. 'Ultimately, we think BaseKit will eventually replace traditional hosting for small business websites,' Best told *Growing Business*, 'and we're working towards that goal.' In 2012, Best became the first Briton to be selected for the prestigious NYC Venture Fellowship in New York, an international programme designed to help entrepreneurs network and establish new overseas offices.

David Langer and Andy Young

Company: GroupSpaces
Young Gun in: 2011 (Ages: 26)
When Silicon Valley veterans Dave McClure and Chris Sacca choose to invest their money in a European start-up, we all sit up and take notice. And, in the case of David Langer and Andy Young's GroupSpaces, our attention is more than justified; the company now boasts members in 80 countries, and was named Company of the Year at the prestigious 'Silicon Valley Comes to the UK' event. GroupSpaces strives to serve all aspects of the groups and societies it manages, from registrations and membership fees to events and activities; an enticing proposition for any group manager, and one that offers huge growth potential. Having also received significant investment from Index Ventures, GroupSpaces is ideally placed to explode in the years to come.

Joshua March

Company: Conversocial
Young Gun in: 2011 (Age: 25)
Growing a business at a rate of 400% during a recession is no mean feat, but Josh March is managing it in style, and confident he can maintain this astonishing upward curve - buoyed by a recent venture capital investment of £1.5m. By 2011, a string of blue-chip multinationals, such as Groupon, ITV, Johnson & Johnson and the London 2012 Olympics organisers, had already signed up for Conversocial's groundbreaking service, which equips users with the tools to manage conversations on social media fan pages. In 2012, the business passed the 100 million mark for social customer service interactions, and had expanded into North America, adding Sephora to its growing client base.

Geoff Watts and Julia Fowler

Company: EDITD (Stylescape)
Young Gun in: 2012 (Ages: 35 and 31)
Former fashion designer Julia Fowler knew the industry needed more factual data to resolve forecasting challenges. So, with co-founder Geoff Watts, she created EDITD, which helps brands and retailers develop better products and price them correctly, advises them when to discount and interprets what consumers are saying. The business won Seedcamp 2010 - a highly regarded investment and mentoring scheme for technology companies across Europe - and in 2011 announced seedfunding of $1.6m led by Index Ventures. EDITD monitors the web, then presents data on an attractively simple dashboard; its easy-to-understand analytics have been a game-changer for fashion buyers, merchandisers, designers and suppliers. The company has clients in the UK, Europe, the US, South Africa, Australia and Asia, and is working with several high-street retailers, who pay a subscription fee determined by the amount of data required.

Chris Tanner and Andrew Mulvenna

Company: Brightpearl
Young Gun in: 2012 (Ages: 32 and 33)
Web-based business management software might not set your heart a-flutter, but the speed of Brightpearl's growth is anything but dull. In a field dominated by industry giants such as Sage, Brightpearl aims to give small businesses access to the same software and insight as large corporates. Users can run all business processes through one piece of software, which covers everything from sales management and inventory control to order purchasing and customer relationship management. The founders originally launched and ran their own skateboarding business, Lush Longboards; however, after becoming frustrated by the limited functionality of business software available, they designed their own. Thus Brightpearl was born, and so far it has secured $6m in investments from Eden Ventures and Notion Capital.

Online consumer services

Ben Hardyment

Company: webflix.co.uk
Young Gun in: 2003 (Age: 32)
Frustrated at the lack of choice at his local Blockbusters, former film director Ben Hardyment decided to use his knowledge of the sector to start a specialist rental service that offers genuine choice in DVD rental. This service became webflix.co.uk, which he sold to LOVEFiLM in 2005. Recently, he secured the largest individual investment ever made on *Dragons' Den*, when Theo Paphitis invested £250,000 in his latest start-up, Zapper. Launched in November 2011 by Hardyment and Mat White, Zapper started as a book-trading website for charities, recyclers and businesses and has grown into a consumer-focused books-for-cash hub.

Nick McCulloch

Company: Nickknows.com
Young Gun in: 2004 (Age: 28)
By the time Nick McCulloch was part of the Young Guns class of 2004, Nickknows.com had enjoyed 80% growth every quarter since its launch from McCulloch's spare room in 2003. Despite being an online offering, McCulloch attributed much of the company's success to its emphasis on offering excellent personal customer service and the ability to 'pick up the phone and talk to someone'.

Imraan Malik

Company: iBetX
Young Gun in: 2004 (Age: 28)
While still in its first full year of trading, iBetX had managed to muscle its way into the thriving but competitive world of betting exchanges. Started with a £3m personal investment from Malik and co-founder Rocky Mirza, iBetX had grown by 90% from 2003 to 2004 and was turning over £7m to £10m a week. iBetX today claims to be the world's fastest growing exchange.

John O'Malia

Company: Trident Gaming
Young Gun in: 2005 (Age: 35)
An online gaming veteran, American O'Malia previously co-founded now defunct spread-betting company IndexTrade, processing bets covering an underlying value of $160m. In July 2003, using the name Betbug, he took betting exchange technology to the US, where sports gambling is largely banned. He acquired betting site Gamebookers, which had an annualised run-rate of €5m profits from revenues of €180m. He remained as CEO of Gamebookers until it was acquired by PartyGaming in August 2006; he subsequently joined the board, but left in 2009 to pursue other business interests.

Nick Mordin

Company: 24-7 Parking
Young Gun in: 2005 (Age: 25)
At the age of 25, Mordin was already a serial entrepreneur. He had started a business at school and sold it by the time he studied banking finance at university. In 2002 he founded 24-7 Parking, taking prime location parking spaces from hotels, supermarkets and private owners, and reselling them to commuters. Accepting online and even mobile bookings, turnover in 2005 was £2.5m.

Cary Marsh

Company: Mydeo
Young Gun in: 2006 (Age: 34)
It was while her partner, Iain Millar, was building a website for their baby Cameron that Marsh realised how easy and cost-effective it was to host personal videos online. Pitched as a more private, ownership-retained alternative to YouTube, Marsh and Millar successfully pitched Mydeo to Microsoft, meaning that the service became the European hosting option on the software giant's Movie Maker product. By 2006, growth stood at 20% per month.

William Berry

Company: AccomodationForStudents.com
Young Gun in: 2006 (Age: 30)
From a germ of an idea when he was a student, by 2006 Berry had established AccomodationForStudents.com as one of the most sophisticated property search sites on the internet. His speedy domination of the niche had secured 10,000 landlords for a £5 fee, effectively blocking off competition. Berry had been keeping himself busy with other interests, too – he had recently sold debt advisers Thomas Charles for £12.5m. Today he owns 75% of debt management firm Vincent Bond & Co. and was co-founder of Film121, which was sold in 2010.

Suranga Chandratillake

Company: Blinkx TV
Young Gun in: 2006 (Age: 28)

People get very excited about bona fide British tech success stories. Yearning for a Facebook or a Twitter of our very own, 'Silicon Roundabout' is watched with eager anticipation for the bursting forth of a Mark Zuckerberg or Jack Dorsey. All the while, though, since long before London's Old Street became synonymous with a buzzy digital start-up scene, Suranga Chandratillake has been building a business that, while remaining relatively low profile, has the world at its feet.

Founded in 2004, Blinkx came into being after the 26-year-old Chandratillake saw the incongruity of a search engine, Google, that focused only on web page searches, omitting online video. Raising £5m in funding, he and his team developed intelligent software that would 'listen' and 'watch' real-time videos and pull them onto his search portal, Blinkx. The engine was based on technology conceived at Cambridge University and that has since been enhanced by $150m in R&D over 12 years. Fox News became the first content partner, with deals with, for example, MTV and Playboy being signed before Chandratillake was named a Young Gun in 2006, still at the age of only 28.

Soon after the 2006 Young Guns were named, Chandratillake led his company through an extremely successful initial public offering (IPO) on the junior stock market, AIM, which rose in the first week of trading to a market cap of $350m. Although he describes the process itself as a 'real distraction', there's no denying it had a huge impact on the company and its future, with revenues doubling year on year since the float.

We decided the time was right to ask for a capital injection.

AIM wasn't the obvious choice, however. Chandratillake explains: 'The business was generating revenue, but if we were to continue . . . on a shoe-string, it would have taken us a very long time to grow. Instead we decided the time was right to ask for a capital injection. Because we were a fast-growth technology company, we really felt venture capital was the obvious option. We started to look into this with Citibank, but after a while they said to us "Look, given you've got a fairly well-defined business, you could go on the stock exchange." And when we looked at the details, we realised it would be a cost-effective way of raising a lot of capital. If we could raise $50m we had a really good plan [of what to do with the money], and that's exactly what we ended up doing.'

Having raised capital, the business also had firm enough foundations to weather the storm when the market got tough in 2008–9. The focus on technology that had always been at the heart of Blinkx meant that the business was operating at a highly developed stage, and had raised capital, before the environment turned difficult. The upshot of this was that, although in 2005 and 2006 there were other start-up companies in the same space as Blinkx, most of them died out, leaving Chandratillake's firm in an extremely strong position when the market started turning rosier in 2009–10.

As with most high-tech companies, profitability was a relatively long time in coming. Before 2010, the company was posting massive losses in the region of $10m to $15m a year, despite a healthy turnover. The market was expecting this to turn around by the end of 2010. In fact, the company first posted a profit at the beginning of the year, months ahead of the plan. 'That was a very exciting time for us,' says Chandratillake. 'It was an amazing feeling as a founder knowing we didn't need to ask for more money. It took a lot of the stress away.'

The AIM float has also allowed the company to grow through acquisitions. It completed two acquisitions in 2011, one of which required a further round of fundraising, which the market provided. The effect of that acquisition was to allow the company to make a 'quantum leap', says Chandratillake. 'Before the acquisition, the company was growing incrementally, whereas overnight we added thousands of distribution partners, and increased the total audience by more than 10 times.' Although acquisitive growth is not a critical part of Blinkx's development strategy, thanks to the healthy profit generated by the company today, opportunities to transform the scale of the business or add huge value will not be ignored.

Today, the company is reaping the benefits of having taken advantage of the fact that, for the last five years, online video has been the fastest growing segment of advertising. It has built a reputation as the remote control for online video, and has built an index of over 35 million hours of searchable video and more than 800 media partnerships, including with national broadcasters, commercial media giants, and private video libraries. Although Chandratillake admits that, because of a difficult 2008, the company hasn't exceeded the expectations some had of it in 2006–7, it has still exhibited convincing growth when compared with the rest of the market. The fact that increasing numbers of people are watching increasing amounts of online video is at the heart of this.

One need only compare the quality of online video when Blinkx launched (mostly amateur, user-generated content) with online video today (with the emergence of iPlayer, Netflix and so on) to appreciate the prescience of Chandratillake's initial idea. And there's plenty left to do. He has recently stood down as CEO, instead focusing on long-term strategy as chairman of the company. 'In our industry you simply can't stand still. No matter how successful you are today, you have to be thinking of tomorrow and the next day. Even in the darkest moments I never questioned what we were doing or the direction we were taking,' says Chandratillake. 'Frankly, it's still early. The vast majority of us watch through regular broadcasting. But the content will be pushed across the internet, and we can be part of the toolkit that lets consumers access that content. The shift has only just started. Only recently have TV advertisers started putting some of their budget into online video. Up until now, it was online advertisers only.'

In our industry you simply can't stand still.

Whatever the future holds – and there are many who think Blinkx is in a prime position to be snapped up by a giant such as Google – Chandratillake is in no doubt of the direction in which our TV-viewing habits are moving, and what this will mean for his business. 'TV will all move online in the next 10 to 15 years. We only need a tiny fraction of that to be a massive company.' Those waiting for Britain's break-out tech success should keep a close eye on Blinkx.

Jerome Touze

Company: Where Are You Now (WAYN)
Young Gun in: 2007 (Age: 27)
Touze and Peter Ward launched travellers' social network site WAYN with £10,000 from Friends Reunited founder Stephen Pankhurst. By 2007, it had secured $11m of institutional backing and Lastminute.com founder Brent Hoberman had become both an investor and company chairman. The site had attracted 9 million users, and revenue was growing by 20% a month. Today the number of users has rocketed to over 20 million, the site has a presence in 193 countries, and revenues and profits have doubled every year since 2010.

Rob Small

Company: Miniclip
Young Gun in: 2007 (Age: 31)
When Small was named a Young Gun in 2007, Miniclip was, after Facebook, the largest privately held website in the world, with 36 million users. Rob Small created the online gaming site in 2001, turning it into a worldwide smash hit with a Dancing Bush game depicting the then US president. Eleven years since its launch, the business is still consistently

profitable and dominates the gaming world. With double the number of players, the site now has more than 65 million users a month and 750 cross-platform games. Its global mission is also being realised, with offices in six countries and games in 17 languages.

Dominic Speakman

Company: Destinology
Young Gun in: 2007 (Age: 31)

Some businesses are self-evidently recession-proof. Debt collection agencies, pawn shops, budget retailers ... perhaps rather extreme examples of businesses for which a floundering economy holds few fears. But tour operators specialising in luxury, tailor-made breaks, one would assume, would at least struggle to thrive when wallets are tightening around the country, and indeed the world. Not so, however, for Destinology, the business founded by 2007 Young Gun Dominic Speakman, which recorded a 2012 turnover of £43m.

Speakman, though only in his twenties when he founded the business, was no rooky. Before the advent of Destinology, and after a stint at PricewaterhouseCoopers in London, he returned to his home town of Bolton and to his father's hugely successful home-based travel agency, Travel Counsellors, of which he became managing director between 2000 and 2003. This proved the perfect launch pad for his own venture, and Destinology was born in 2004.

Since then, Speakman has retained 100% equity and has managed to increase profits every year of the business's existence. The company has grown its offering slowly but sustainably. In 2004, with five staff, sales focused on four destinations: Dubai, the Maldives, Mauritius and Thailand. The Caribbean and USA were added in 2005, when turnover had reached £6.6m, and by the time Speakman was a 2007 Young Gun, turnover was at £15m, destinations offered were multiple and worldwide, and the company was named fourteenth in *The Sunday Times* 100 Best Small Companies to Work For list. Today it sells over 10,000 luxury holidays each year and in 2012 employed 95 people.

One important area where he has been successful is the elimination of unnecessary costs. From day one, Speakman has cut out the middleman at all stages, and Destinology deals directly with hotels and airlines. He has also concentrated on reducing marketing costs as much as possible, particularly through a £1m search and marketing campaign he describes as 'cost-effective' which has had valuable search engine optimisation (SEO) results, ensuring that Destinology ranks highly for valuable phrases such as 'luxury European holidays'. He also explains that 'targeted PR and marketing, particularly through broadcast partners such as *X Factor* and *Britain & Ireland's Next Top Model* has reached new customers'; these tend to be drawn in by the cost (Speakman says that strong links with hotels and resorts worldwide mean the company can beat competitors on value) and the company's focus on customer service. And thanks to strong sales, partner-funded marketing has tended to be easy to attract, with hotels and airlines keen to invest in activities targeted to the company's database.

The Bolton-based tour operator has also won valuable (and inexpensive) PR through awards, the most recent of which include being named Best Weddings and Honeymoons Tour Operator, Best Operator to the Indian Ocean and Best Tour Operator to the Middle East in the medium-sized category at the 2012 British Travel Awards. A growing list of celebrity clients also helps matters.

The company's ability to be flexible has played an important part in helping it navigate choppy economic waters. One important shift was Speakman's decision to add short-haul flights to the company's offering. He explains: 'The addition of short-haul holidays enabled customers either to opt for a lower-cost holiday if desired, or, more usually, to take a second or third annual break with us, adding shorter breaks to their annual holiday booking.' He also credits a focus on proprietary technology for setting the company apart: 'Investing in technology from day one has proved hugely successful. Developing our resource in-house and building our own proprietary software, rather than outsourcing, has allowed us to stay ahead of the competition.'

Investing in technology from day one has proved hugely successful.

Staying ahead means that the company is looking forward at moving into new markets, with cruising being singled out as one field in which

Destinology can excel. According to Speakman, this area is well suited to the business's current client base and also offers the potential to reach new customers. 'Another short-term goal is to start working with the travel trade,' he says, 'selling through agents as well as continuing to sell direct to the customer ... Longer term, we will also look at overseas expansion and a second office to handle ground arrangements and offer holidays to a new resident market.' He describes his growth plans as 'ambitious', and although the company has grown entirely from profits until now, he is open to looking at external funding should it be required for Destinology to fulfil its potential.

For a company just nine years old, Speakman has a lot to be proud of. Yet it is its record of staff retention that gives him most satisfaction, he says. Members of the founding team still work at Destinology today. It is obviously a vote of confidence in the company as a place to work, but keeping hold of staff who have built up expertise makes sound business sense, and, he says, has played a key part in Destinology being able to offer the customer service on which it has built its reputation.

In 2011, the company was included by *The Telegraph* in its list of small firms that are set to be the foundation of the UK's recovery, and with impressive growth plans in the pipeline, Speakman seems determined to ensure that the business continues its upward trajectory. By helping legions of Brits get away to a spot of luxury, Destinology remains a company that's going places.

Ryan Notz

Company: MyBuilder
Young Gun in: 2008 (Age: 33)
Former stonemason Notz knows how hard it can be for tradespeople to find steady work. Sick of agencies sending him out to jobs that didn't match his skills, he set up MyBuilder, which allows consumers to post jobs online that tradespeople can bid for. Originally self-funded, Notz won European-wide funding competition Seedcamp, securing €50,000 and mentoring for a 10% stake. He then netted a further £500,000 from investors such as Bebo co-founder Paul Birch and construction giant Travis Perkins, and in 2009 Channel 4's 4iP fund acquired a minority equity stake for £350,000. Trading since October 2007, more than 14,000 jobs are listed every month, and over 60,000 tradespeople are registered across the UK.

Sokratis Papafloratos

Company: TrustedPlaces
Young Gun in: 2009 (Age: 30)
TrustedPlaces initially provided user-generated reviews for restaurants, bars, pubs and clubs. However, steady growth saw the company, co-founded in 2006 by Sokratis Papafloratos, add ratings of everything from sport and leisure clubs to shops and hotels. With membership and revenues growing quickly, it perhaps is no surprise that the business was snapped up by Yell in 2010. Papafloratos worked at Yell as head of social products until 2011.

Kieran O'Neill

Company: Playfire
Young Gun in: 2009 (Age: 21)
Founding a social network for gamers and guiding it through a $1m round of seed backing (from the likes of Bebo founder Michael Birch and former Sony chairman Chris Deering) would be considered precocious for most 21-year-olds. Playfire, however, is O'Neill's third business. Having already sold HolyLemon.com, the video-sharing site he built at the age of 15, for $1.25m, he then co-founded PSU.com, the largest PlayStation community in the world, before setting up his latest venture with Ben Phillips and Seb Hayes. In total, the business raised $3.1m in funding and grew to 1.2 million gamers using the product before it was acquired by Green Man Gaming for an undisclosed sum.

Michael Phillips

Company: ConsumerChoices.co.uk
Young Gun in: 2010 (Age: 34)
Price comparison websites have changed the way people buy. ConsumerChoices.co.uk, set up in 2005, has made the most of this fact and by 2010 had become the largest Ofcom-accredited comparison website in the UK. It helps UK consumers save money across 10 areas - including broadband, home phone, gas and electricity, and insurance. It's also involved in powering leading websites such as GoCompare.com, Comparethemarket.com and Confused.com, as well as around 30 other partners.

It achieved a turnover in 2012 of almost £11m, and successfully expanded into Spain, France and Germany. Profitable since day one, the business secured a £10m investment from government-backed scheme the Business Growth Fund in August 2012, which it plans to use to fund further international growth. In the same year, it also saw success at *The Sunday Times* 2012 Tech Track 100 Awards, where it was named one of the UK's fastest growing companies for the second year running.

Tim Morgan

Company: Picklive
Young Gun in: 2010 (Age: 34)
Picklive was less than a year old when its founder, Tim Morgan, was named a 2010 Young Gun. The site allows subscribers to play against each other in real time while watching live football – a concept that impressed investor Stefan Glaenzer so much that he led on a six-figure sum in a seedfunding round. In July 2010, Morgan made a successful exit after selling the company to a group of private investors led by David Galan, CEO of pool betting firm Sports Millions. He has since gone on to launch his latest venture, Summer Chimney Wine Club.

Jason Trost

Company: Smarkets
Young Gun in: 2010 (Age: 29)
Smarkets has made online trading simple and has attracted a niche crowd betting on a wide range of activities which include, among other things, politics, entertainment and current affairs. A sizeable investment led by ex-Last.fm chairman Stefan Glaenzer has helped it grow to its current state. The site reached the landmark of surpassing £100m in trading volume in 2012, and has launched a mobile site to keep visitors coming through a variety of media.

Henry Erskine Crum and Alexander Will

Company: Spoonfed Media
Young Gun in: 2011 (Ages: 28)
If it's happening in London, you can bet that Henry Erskine Crum and Alexander Will have heard about it. The co-founders of Spoonfed Media, and publishers of spoonfed.co.uk, know the capital like the backs of their hands, and have painstakingly established contact with a phalanx of owners, promoters and organisers who are all too happy to promote their bars and clubs on Spoonfed's pages. It's now listing 30,000 events per month, and has seen unique users grow 25% month on month since 2009. Crum and Will, who met as students at the London School of Economics, have also launched bullseyehub.com, a SaaS platform for event organisers to manage all their online event marketing.

David Grimes and Paul Haydock

Company: myParcelDelivery.com
Young Gun in: 2011 (Ages: 28)
David Grimes and Paul Haydock graduated from Cambridge University in 2006, and this is already their second start-up. myParcelDelivery.com has partnered with courier companies such as UPS, TNT and DHL so that users (be they businesses, eBay sellers or the general public) can book and pay for the shipping of parcels through its website at a cheaper rate than if they went direct to the brands themselves. The Manchester-based start-up secured a six-figure funding injection from a private investor in 2011, and were predicting a 2012 turnover of £5m. In addition to growing their company's brand and online presence, they intend to expand into European markets. 'We have achieved a lot for such a young company; however, we are hungry for more. There's still a lot we're aspiring to, and the next year promises to see big things happening for myParcelDelivery.com,' the entrepreneurs told *Growing Business* in 2011.

Ian Hogarth, Pete Smith and Michelle You

Company: Songkick
Young Gun in: 2011 (Ages: 29)
Songkick is only four years old but today is the second largest concert site on the internet after Ticketmaster. The concept, devised by Ian Hogarth, Pete Smith and Michelle You, is based around making going to concerts as easy as it is to go to the movies. Songkick tracks users' favourite artists by creating personalised alerts and calendars. The site saw an impressive 800% growth in traffic in 2010, and the founders are hoping to see it become the largest online concert service.

To this end, it has partnered with brands including Bandcamp, BBC, foursquare, VEVO, Warner Music Group and YouTube. From the user's point of view, the service interprets your taste preferences handily with Last FM, Pandora and iTunes. Private investment in the start-up so far has totalled $2m, and the founders are now focusing on innovation in order to grow the service into a sustainable, and highly profitable, business. As music-streaming services gain traction it has become easier and easier to check out a new artist, whether they are from Sao Paulo, San Francisco or Cape Town, and Songkick's mobile products such as its iPhone app help fans keep track on the go.

Anthony Eskinazi

Company: Park At My House
Young Gun in: 2011 (Age: 28)
It has been ever thus: where some see inconvenience and frustration, others see simple supply and demand-based entrepreneurial opportunity. Finding a parking space causes more than its fair share of angst, so Eskinazi hit on the idea of letting people advertise their unused private parking spaces for hire. The site's users can advertise, or use it to find spaces nearby. After two years of organic growth, the company took on a significant investment from BMW, no less, which will allow it to grow aggressively, according to its founder. This recent partnership marks a major breakthrough for the business, and now it has reached profitability, the focus is on international growth as well as the launch of mobile services.

Tom Valentine

Company: Secret Escapes
Young Gun in: 2012 (Age: 31)
Even the most luxurious hotels don't like having empty rooms. It is this plain fact that makes Secret Escapes, founded in 2010, such a great proposition for both customers and hotel and holiday suppliers alike. Secret Escapes negotiates exclusive rates for luxury hand-picked hotels and holidays in the UK and abroad at up to 70% off the price you'd pay by booking anywhere else. The founding team has been able to bring extensive digital start-up knowledge and experience to the venture, with Valentine having worked at eBay and Seatwave, and co-founders Alex Saint and Troy Collins from Dealchecker. Investors have flocked to become involved, and include Octopus Ventures, Atlas Ventures, Robin Klein (Index), Alex Chesterman (Zoopla), Andy McLoughlin (Huddle) and Sokratis Papafloratis (TrustedPlaces).

Since being named a 2012 Young Gun, Valentine's Secret Escapes has received a further £8m investment from existing investors Octopus Ventures and Atlas Venture in a funding round led by Index Ventures. The company, which experienced an astonishing 1,400% growth in the 12 months prior to August 2012, is set to use the latest instalment to fund global expansion.

Vinay Gupta and Tom Wright

Company: WhipCar
Young Gun in: 2012 (Ages: 31 and 33)
Since 2010, the neighbour-to-neighbour car rental service has connected car owners who don't drive their car all the time with safe, approved drivers nearby. WhipCar was the first service of its kind in the world and membership is free for both car owners and drivers. There are now over 19,000 car owners across the UK renting out their cars and 90% of Londoners are within a 10-minute walk of a WhipCar. Vinay Gupta met co-founder Tom Wright while working as a digital media strategist for Fleming Media, where Wright was an employee at the time. The idea behind WhipCar, when it came, felt to them 'too big to ignore'. They are now globally recognised speakers championing the sharing economy and their ambition to turn the car from a product into a managed service. In 2012, the European Commission campaign launched to combat climate

change chose the company to represent the UK and has provided a case study of WhipCar on its website as an example of an eco-friendly business.

Greg Marsh and Tim Davey

Company: onefinestay
Young Gun in: 2012 (Ages: 33 and 35)
The concept is getting investors excited. Since its launch in 2010, onefinestay has raised a total of $16m, and in June 2012 the company secured $12m in a funding round led by Canaan Partners - a deal also involving existing investors Index Ventures and PROfounders Capital. Why the enthusiasm? onefinestay's model allows people to let out their homes to travellers seeking a 'more authentic local experience' - but without skimping on the luxury. Each of the 600 homes listed on the site has been curated by the team for unique character and exceptional quality and guests can expect to receive hotel-style services that even include an iPhone and 24/7 support from the dedicated guest services team. Flush from its success in London, onefinestay New York launched in May 2012, the first step in the founders' wider ambitions for international expansion.

Felix Leuschner

Company: Stylistpick
Young Gun in: 2012 (Age: 30)
Stylistpick is an online-only fashion brand focused on delivering its customers shoes with the wow factor, the perfect handbag, and the most amazing statement jewellery handpicked by celebrity stylists. Launched in November 2010, Stylistpick has acquired more than 850,000 members to date and recently expanded to France and Spain. With $7m raised in series A venture capital funding, followed by $11m series B from venture capital funds Index Ventures, Accel Partners and Fidelity Growth Partners Europe, growth has been rapid. And bagging an exclusive design collaboration with UK style icon Cheryl Cole has surely helped.

James Street and Neil Waller

Company: My Destination
Young Gun in: 2012 (Ages: 27 and 28)
Attracting around 18 million annual visitors, My Destination is a network of travel sites providing advice and information that is curated exclusively by local experts. The co-founders, who met at university, initially launched a site for a holiday resort in Spain, but quickly realised the potential and expanded the business using a franchise model. Now, their site spans over 58 countries and covers more than 120 destinations worldwide, with each territory being run by a team on the ground. Franchisees pay a fee to buy their territory and receive a split of royalties. The business has seen 255% growth year on year and has around 250 people working within the group.

Recruitment

Charlie Osmond

Company: FreshMinds
Young Gun in: 2003 (Age: 26)
Straight out of university, Cambridge alumni Charlie Osmond and Caroline Plumb wasted no time in setting up student research company FreshMinds in 2000. By 2004 the company employed 15 and had a regular pool of PhD and MA students carrying out research on behalf of clients as notable as Unilever, Diageo and HSBC. In that year, when Osmond was still only 26, *Growing Business* described the duo as 'quickly becoming the faces of young entrepreneurial Britain'. That's quite an epithet to live up to, but although the Fresh Group, as the firm is now known, has never shown the kind of stratospheric growth demonstrated by businesses of some other Young Guns, its understated success provides a sterling example of how to diversify into other services, and how to grow a sustainable, profitable and productive firm.

For that reason, Osmond and Plumb have since been called upon to represent young entrepreneurial Britain. Plumb, for example, was among a group of eminent businesspeople selected to be part of a UK Trade & Investment (UKTI) delegation to promote UK exports and investment in India in 2010. She has also been named twice on *Management Today's* list of '35 under 35' businesswomen, sits on the board of the Saïd Business School in Oxford, and is a council member of the Small Business Forum. Osmond, meanwhile, was named Young Entrepreneur of the Year by *Esquire* magazine in 2007, and other accolades include London Entrepreneur of the Year.

The company that so impressed has morphed from FreshMinds into Fresh Group. The original venture, FreshMinds Research, spawned two sister companies: FreshMinds Talent and FreshNetworks. Clients working with the research firm, impressed by the calibre of the people they came across, began asking if FreshMinds could help them find equally talented individuals. FreshMinds Talent (which recently opened an office in Scotland) was formed to do exactly this. And, explains Osmond, 'In 2007-8 we were doing more and more research using social relations as a way to gather data. We thought there's so much opportunity in this space.' Osmond then went to work on what would become social media consultancy FreshNetworks.

The developing group was given a strong vote of confidence in 2008 when it won the Bank of Scotland Corporate Entrepreneur Challenge, an award that brought with it up to £5m in funding for FreshNetworks. The company triumphed over a shortlist of firms including Gü Chocolate Puds, Quintessentially and Country House Weddings Group. The founding partners impressed the judges by explaining the opportunity for the fledgling FreshNetworks to help large brands understand and communicate with their customers through online communities, as market research increasingly goes online, rather than being run through focus groups.

Today, FreshNetworks consists of a team of around 35 and designs and delivers digital and social strategies for global brands including Telefónica O2, Jimmy Choo and Sage. In going after the world-leading brands, it has followed the strategy set by FreshMinds from day one: always to target the biggest names. To anyone who believes that small firms struggle to attract large clients, FreshMinds is a firm rebuttal. 'There are certain bits of work we couldn't do because, say, we didn't have 400 people who could all start working on a particular project tomorrow, but it hasn't really been a challenge. People quite like the fact we're a focused group with high standards,' says Osmond. 'We wanted clients who would push us and make sure we were at the top of our game.'

People like the fact we're a focused group with high standards.

Being at the top of their game has meant that the group's turnover has risen from £1.5m in 2003 when Osmond was named a Young Gun to around £11m today, and staff numbers have grown to over 100. However, risks associated with growth, and particularly with diversifying into new revenue streams, were not insignificant. Osmond names one they did not expect: when a founder goes and launches a new business – as he did when FreshNetworks was conceived – it can lead to uncertainty among staff of the existing business. 'I was surprised,' he says, 'when people started asking "Does this mean you care less about the bit of the business

I'm in?"' Navigating this successfully, Osmond and Plumb have now appointed a managing director for FreshNetworks, as well as managing directors for FreshMinds Research and FreshMinds Talent. This started the conversation about the extent to which the businesses should be integrated, or whether to let them develop at their own pace and form their own distinct cultures, a conversation Osmond admits is 'ongoing'.

Unlike many service-based firms, the Fresh Group has survived the economic climate with some aplomb. Having a social media consultancy as one of the core revenue streams has helped with this. 'It's a fast-growing market,' says Osmond, and one that has changed even since FreshNetworks was founded, as potential clients catch up with the significance of social media for their businesses - meaning that although there's more competition, there's also more available budget. Recruitment, however, has proved slightly more of a challenge, and according to Osmond, has demonstrated some interesting behaviours. 'So, for instance, you might have the exact same number of clients as you did the year before, but there's a huge difference when you get through the interviews; either the bar will suddenly get higher and they get more picky, or they would suddenly put off the role. In recruitment, that's a massive challenge, as we get paid when the person is in their job. If the role gets put off for two months, they might have moved on by then, and we have to do twice the amount of work [by filling the role a second time].'

We have always tried to create somewhere we're proud of and from where people get a lot of satisfaction and great careers.

The group has always grown organically, and remaining privately owned has meant that Osmond and Plumb have always taken the business in exactly the direction they wanted. Areas of investment have been defined to a large extent by what the duo find interesting and exciting, admits Osmond: 'Even now we find ourselves saying "Do we want to do this? Or this, which may be harder but more fun."' It also means they could prioritise things that were important to them when they first started soon after graduating. This has played a large part in the company being named as one of the UK's best places to work in 2010 and 2011. Being a good place to work is 'incredibly important', says Osmond. 'We have always tried to create somewhere we're proud of and from where people get a lot of satisfaction and great careers. We have achieved that because it was something we cared about, because we were two idealistic 21-year-olds to whom that was important.'

Helen Stokes

Company: Morgan Hunt
Young Gun in: 2006 (Age: 34)
Recruitment in the sometimes slow-moving and red tape-strewn public sector is a challenge Stokes approached with relish. By taking a long-term view and building the Morgan Hunt brand, rather than making quick profits, Stokes was impressive in taking on the big players following the company's creation in 2002. Before leaving the company in October 2010, she had built staff numbers to over 200, opened offices in London, Birmingham and Manchester, as well as overseas operations in Moscow and St Petersburg, and had achieved a turnover of £88m in 2009-10.

Paul King

Company: G2 Recruitment
Young Gun in: 2006 (Age: 35)
'So far,' says James Gorfin, co-founder of G2 Recruitment, 'we've been recession-proof.' And then some. The founding trio of Gorfin, Paul King and Simon Gillings were named Young Guns in 2006, when their fledgling firm was projected to hit a turnover of £11m. Only six years later, and it's climbed to over £50m.

Like many a successful entrepreneur, Gorfin puts the credit to this firmly with his employees. But unlike most entrepreneurs, when he talks of the importance of people - hiring the right ones and investing in them - it's not just empty rhetoric. Instead it's a fundamental cornerstone of how G2 Recruitment has grown so quickly and so sustainably. Almost all of their 90 plus staff have been hired at graduate level. 'We did hire one manager,' says Gorfin, 'but that was a one-off.'

The company then invests heavily in training and development to ensure that there are always enough people to step up to the next level. The growth of G2 is in this way intrinsically linked to the performance of the staff. New offices are opened only when there's somebody the company feels is ready for the responsibility of running their own office.

This leads to potentially life-changing opportunities for employees. One member of staff recently moved to Houston, Texas, to open a new office. Around a quarter of G2's business comes from oil and gas recruitment, making it a strategically important base for the business. 'Houston is the oil and gas capital of the world,' Gorfin notes. 'It was a bit of a gamble as it was an untested marketplace – we hadn't done much business there previously – but we decided to take a calculated risk, especially as we had someone who was desperate to live there.'

We decided to take a calculated risk.

The company also has branches in Manchester and London, alongside the Bristol headquarters. It also has two subsidiary companies in London – no surprises that they are being run by previous staff members. One of these companies, Vivid Resourcing, is in fact run by Charlie Walker, who himself went on to become a Young Gun in 2011.

The G2 founders are now full steam ahead with launching new branches around the world. A Netherlands office recently opened and Norway and Germany are other territories under consideration. However, because G2 works with clients worldwide, there are multiple countries in which an office could be extremely successful. Gorfin notes that there would be nothing really stopping the company expanding in Asia, for example, in the imminent future. 'We can't open too many at once,' he says, pointing out that ensuring there's an employee ready for the level of responsibility their own office would entail can take some time. It's unusual perhaps to have the level of expansion dictated by people, rather than cashflow, but it's a strategy that's paying dividends.

All expansion so far has been funded through profits. 'We're an entirely self-funded business,' says Gorfin. 'We've never even asked for a bank loan. External capital isn't something we particularly want to do, and we've never needed to do it.' Keeping control is understandably a priority, but, says Gorfin pragmatically, 'Of course, if someone came along with a great proposal, we'd look at it.'

Although relatively large now, the business has maintained a start-up's flexibility. It is this, perhaps, that has played the largest part in its indomitability in the face of a double-dip recession. 'We did have some people doing public sector recruitment, for example,' explains Gorfin, 'but when the Conservatives came in we moved them out of that. We can do that easily.' The company has avoided putting all its eggs in one basket by ensuring that it's not overly reliant on one client, or even one sector or one area of the world. The oil and gas sector's buoyancy makes up for slower times elsewhere, for example. And Gorfin explains: 'We do business overseas in places like Canada, Singapore and even Africa. These places aren't experiencing the same problems as the UK and Europe.'

That has been combined with old-fashioned competency and - of course - a strong team. 'If you know what you're doing, day in, day out, and you have people who know what they're doing, then you can grow,' says Gorfin. The plan now is to open a couple of offices a year. 'In recruitment,

There's no limit to our beliefs about our potential.

it's sometimes difficult to know where we'll be in six months' time, never mind in five years,' says Gorfin. 'But if we keep growing at the rate we are doing, we'll have eight, nine or ten new offices overseas, which will be fantastic.'

This is by no means the extent of the founders' ambition, though. Gorfin points to a more established competitor turning over in the region of £500m, and still growing. He is sure they can emulate such scale, if they keep going about things the right way. 'There's no limit to our beliefs about our potential.'

Robert Leggett

Company: Omni Resource Management Solutions
Young Gun in: 2007 (Age: 35)
By providing a start-to-end recruitment service for clients recruiting from 50 to 750 people a year, Leggett managed to grow carbon-neutral Cheshire company Omni from a £30,000 personal overdraft to become a business that by 2007 was turning over £16m. The company, of which Leggett is now chairman, is looking to grow still further, and to that end recently opened new offices in Manchester and London.

Tom Savage

Companies: Bright Green Talent, Blue Ventures, Make Your Mark with a Tenner, Tiptheplanet.com
Young Gun in: 2007 (Age: 27)
In 2003, Tom Savage and Alasdair Harris set up Blue Ventures, running marine conservation trips to Madagascar. By 2007 it was making about £350,000 a year and had won two UN prizes, responsible travel awards and an award worth £140,000. Savage had also set up a 'wiki' for submitting eco-friendly tips called Tip The Planet, launched Make Your Mark with a Tenner with Oli Barrett and sat on the board of Young Enterprise London. Bright Green Talent, which he co-founded with Paul Hannam, was a recruitment agency which focused on helping companies with a CSR or environmental agenda recruit and retain talented staff. The company has since been renamed Savage & Hall and Savage consults to businesses, government agencies and not-for-profits as well as being a regular speaker and writer.

Sumon Sadhu

Company: Snaptalent
Young Gun in: 2008 (Age: 25)
The first ever intern at Library House, Sumon Sadhu has also consulted for the government on enterprise policy, set up Europe's largest tech entrepreneurship society and sat on the advisory board of Seedcamp. He abandoned his PhD to help set up Snaptalent in the US, after being headhunted by Paul Graham of the prestigious Y Combinator fund. Using controversial IP targeting, Snaptalent aimed to disrupt the way in which online recruitment ads are distributed, with relevant job ads appearing where prospects spend their time on the web. However, the company closed in 2009, saying the model 'ended up being economically unviable as a business. Primarily because the number of candidate leads generated per impression wasn't able to satisfy employers to keep buying and therefore for publishers to keep getting paid.' Sadhu went on to become director of intelligence at Silicon Valley consultancy Quid.

Jamie Woods

Company: JCW
Young Gun in: 2011 (Age: 28)
Things weren't looking good for recruitment firm JCW in 2008, when its entire client base was made up of banking and financial organisations – a sector that didn't exactly remain unscathed by the recession. The fact that it recovered to see high growth of both profits and turnover in 2009 is testament to its resilience and ability to adapt, as well as the determination of 28-year-old founder Jamie Woods.

With JCW currently operating as supplier of choice to a number of FTSE 100 organisations, introducing risk management, regulatory compliance and audit professionals, the company opened a New York office in March 2012. Woods' overall strategy will take the business past the 100-employee mark in 2014.

Charlie Walker

Company: Vivid Resourcing
Young Gun in: 2011 (Age: 27)
IT recruitment isn't a sector to get the pulse racing, so how do you create something different, a bit exciting, as well as solid and effective? A projected 2012 turnover of £12m helps. Vivid Resourcing was three years old in 2011, and had seen the third highest compound growth rate of any recruitment business in the UK. Charlie Walker's achievement is all the more impressive when it's taken into account that in 2009 the NHS made up 65% of Vivid Resourcing's business – and this was reduced to 15% with no pause in growth.

Saying that, Walker admits that the economic climate of the last few years has been his biggest obstacle: 'Our marketplace shifted dramatically to give our end clients more power at the negotiating table.' Furthermore, a number of clients have gone into administration, meaning savvy handling of cashflow has been critical. Despite this, the firm is flying and European expansion is under way.

Lucian Tarnowski

Company: BraveNewTalent
Young Gun in: 2011 (Age: 27)
Having expanded into the US and India, and trebled the size of his team, Lucian Tarnowski had a busy 2011. His business, BraveNewTalent, is cutting a swathe through the recruitment sector with its groundbreaking offering, which allows employers to engage and develop people through social media Talent Communities.

Companies such as Tesco, L'Oréal and Channel 4 have all signed up to use the site, and having secured investment from Northzone Ventures, BraveNewTalent is poised to expand further in the months ahead. Lucian is already a member of the Young Global Leaders at the World Economic Forum, and is set for further accolades on the back of BraveNewTalent's success.

Adrian Kinnersley

Company: Twenty Recruitment
Young Gun in: 2012 (Age: 34)
Founded in 2009, Twenty Recruitment is attempting to carve a niche in the world of recruitment by being genuinely value driven, and focusing on careers, not just jobs. Its rapid rate of growth so far attests to the wisdom of this strategy: 2011 turnover increased by over £3m to reach £7m, and £12m is predicted in 2013. A New York office was opened in 2011, and UK growth is now being replicated Stateside. It is perhaps no surprise that this venture is proving incredibly successful; co-founders Kinnersley and Paul Marsden sold their previous recruitment firm, Astbury Marsden, for £17.5m in 2007.

Lyndsey Simpson

Company: The Curve Group
Young Gun in: 2012 (Age: 34)
Simpson had established herself as a high-flyer in the world of financial services when she bought into recruitment service The Curve Group in 2007, and has led the company from a turnover of £405,000 to over £2m. She was also responsible for signing up 20 new clients within a year, and

launched a new division that became profitable within four months. Offering outsourcing services and providing guidance to employers searching for the perfect candidate, as well as support for the job seeker, the company's clients include HSBC, Reiss, Balfour Beatty, RBS, Virgin, KPMG, The National Trust, Aston Villa FC and Barclays.

Clare Johnston

Company: Up Group
Young Gun in: 2012 (Age: 31)
By focusing purely on the digital and online field, Clare Johnston's executive search and networking firm has found a lucrative niche in a fast-growing area. Johnston launched the company at the age of 26 with £40,000 of her own money (having declined external funding), and has since grown it to a profitable £2m business. Adopting a differentiated strategy from the outset, Up Group focused on creating an exclusive talent network and hosting invite-only events for those involved in the digital ecosystem: investors, entrepreneurs and senior executives from start-ups to corporates. Up Group builds the leadership teams of companies, often helping US firms launch into Europe and UK businesses to expand overseas. It has worked with some of the most exciting names in digital, including eBay, Google, Paddy Power, eHarmony, Spotify, Wonga, Mind Candy, Moo, Just Eat . . . the list goes on and on. Overseas offices are planned.

Lee Biggins and Brian Wakem

Company: CV Library
Young Gun in: 2012 (Ages: 34 and 32)
With over 5 million CVs in CV Library's database, it's no wonder clients such as G4S, Asda and TK Maxx, plus recruitment agencies, are using the job board to fill vacancies. The Hampshire-based firm, founded in 2000, employs 55 staff, turned over £4.7m in 2011, and is projected to grow that to £6.7m in 2012 - during the last five years, the career website has grown by 427%. The business was named the Best Career Site at the Website of the Year Awards 2012.

Founders Biggins and Wakem are now looking at new ways to enhance clients' recruitment campaigns through, for example, social media profiles and mobile solutions.

Retail

Michael Ross

Company: figleaves.com
Young Gun in: 2003 (Age: 34)
Chief executive Ross joined online lingerie retailer figleaves.com in 1999 after five years at McKinsey. Under his stewardship, it started to realise its potential, making £7.2m in 2003. No longer at figleaves.com, Ross has gone on to co-found e-commerce advisory firm eCommera, and among his positions is advisory board member at Glasses Direct. In 2011 he ranked number 27 on *Retail Week*'s ranking of the 50 most influential people in retail.

Stephen Hall

Company: Gamestation
Young Gun in: 2003 (Age: 34)
It took a £3,000 Prince's Trust loan to get video and computer games retailer Gamestation up and running back in 1993. But in less than 10 years founders Stephen Hall and Julian Gladwin turned the company into a 450-strong team, with 74 stores around the UK and a turnover of £35m to April 2002. Hall left the company in 2003 after its sale to Blockbuster.

Thea Green

Company: Nails Inc
Young Gun in: 2003 (Age: 27)
If you were asked to bet on the success of a 24-year-old launching her first business - a nail bar - you'd have been forgiven for keeping a tight hold of your money. But in 1999, Thea Green, then working as a fashion editor in London, saw a gap on the British high street. In New York at that time, a manicure was an integral part of many women's grooming regimes.

People - usually professional women with little time to spare - could pop into nail bars on main streets around the city for an affordable pampering session. The same opportunity did not exist in London. Green started Nails Inc with £250,000 and, having developed a product range for her budding venture, opened the first Nails Inc salon, near London's Bond Street, to queues stretching down the street. The '15-minute manicure' she developed became an instant hit - and the product range has grown and thrived ever since.

By the time Nails Inc was four years old, Green became one of the first ever Young Guns. She had already opened around 30 salons, could count the likes of Kylie Minogue as customers, and the business turned over around £3.5m the previous year. Signs were good, but even then, few would have predicted the extent of the business's growth in the following years. Turnover in 2012 was set to hit a cool £22m. The business has 56 concessions in UK stores such as Selfridges, House of Fraser, Debenhams and Harvey Nichols. Already trading in Ireland, Hong Kong, North America and Canada, Green is now busy exploring opportunities in South Africa, Asia and Australia. With all this, it's no surprise the entrepreneur - also a mum of three - received an MBE for services to the beauty industry in 2011.

As a decided non-essential, it at first seems remarkable that a business selling nail varnish and salon services could thrive to such an extent during these times of austerity. But, as the 'lipstick index' testifies, firms that provide an affordable yet luxurious pick-me-up can thrive in tough economic times; a bottle of Nails Inc nail varnish costs around £10. Green has also ensured that the brand has built and maintained a fashion-forward, youthful image. Her fashion background was integral in the creation of the product range - with all the shades inspired by the latest catwalk trends, and frequent collaborations with designers meaning that the products are bang up to date. Innovation is key, with special effects such as magnetic, 3D glitter, crackle and nail jewellery appealing to fashion-conscious consumers eager to experiment, while earning the firm valuable column inches. The business has also benefited from a seemingly instinctive marketing savvy: all the products, for example, are instantly identifiable by being named after famous London destinations (Shoreditch, for example, is hot pink, while St James is pillar-box red).

Nails Inc salons today number 58 nationwide. The firm has two standalone stores, but its nail bars are predominantly found in department stores across the UK and Ireland, including Harvey Nichols, Selfridges,

House of Fraser, Debenhams, John Lewis and Boots, a clever decision that allows customers to take advantage of its manicure services in the most convenient locations. Nails Inc has established itself as the UK's most successful and popular nail bar chain, seeing on average 10,000 customers per week.

It's hardly surprising that Green has ambitions beyond the UK. In 2011, the business launched internationally, and it did so in a huge way. Turnover rocketed in 2012, as the cosmetics giant Sephora took on all of Nails Inc's products in its stores around the world. It launched first in 50 Sephora stores in the USA, which made a huge impact, but already the business has a significant global presence. Green now has her eye on the huge Asian market, as well as Australia and the Middle East.

Nails are big business. Thea Green spotted that fact while still only in her early 20s, and as a result her firm stands on the brink of world domination.

Nina Hampson

Company: Myla
Young Gun in: 2003 (Age: 30)
Described as 'Prada with a hard-on', upmarket lingerie and sex toys outfit Myla swiftly attracted a cult clientele, including Victoria Beckham and Kate Moss. Founders Hampson and Charlotte Semler met on a three-month Tesco brand strategy project and decided to start a business. Myla is one of the UK's leading luxury lingerie brands, with 12 boutiques and concessions. The business also has a thriving online, mail order and wholesale business.

Nasa Khan

Company: The Accessory People
Young Gun in: 2003 (Age: 30)
Khan was prominent in *The Sunday Times* Rich List in 2003 with a worth of £45m. He started his mobile accessory business, The Accessory People, with just £2,000 from friends in 1995, and by 2003 it had a turnover of £450m. However, Khan's fate took a dramatic turn for the worse when he was jailed for nine years in 2011 after being convicted of tax fraud.

Serena Rees

Company: Agent Provocateur
Young Gun in: 2003 (Age: 34)
Rees and co-founder Joseph Corre held up two fingers to British prudishness and set up shop in 1994 with the launch of high-class lingerie outfit Agent Provocateur. By 2003 it was a cult brand with six stores. Rees exited in 2007 when the business was bought by private equity house 3i for £60m. She went on to co-found fashionable London bakery Cocomaya.

Michael Acton Smith

Company: Firebox/Mind Candy
Young Gun in: 2003 (Age: 28)

Groundbreaking. Game-changing. Disruptive. These words are bandied around with some frequency when talking about the start-up scene. Rarely, however, are they genuinely justified, and much more rarely are they used to describe businesses that essentially make kids' games. Enter Moshi Monsters. If you haven't heard of it, ten to one you don't have young children. It's fair to say that among this demographic, Moshi Monsters is a bona fide phenomenon. A social gaming concept based on cute collectable critters, it has 65 million users in 150 countries, has inspired its own TV station, magazine and music label, and the business behind it, Mind Candy, has been tipped by some to be 'Europe's next billion-dollar break-out success'. As a result, Mind Candy's founder, Michael Acton Smith, is gaining a certain amount of celebrity, recently appearing on the cover of *Wired* magazine. But in 2003, when he was named a Young Gun, he hadn't yet even launched Mind Candy. Instead, his business Firebox was impressing with its innovative products and fast growth.

Web gadget shop Firebox was three years old in 2003, and had raised £75,000 at the height of the dotcom boom. The company was 20-person strong, profitable, and was turning over £8m. One particular product Acton Smith and co-founder Tom Boardman devised, shot chess (which gave chess a less salubrious edge by turning it into a drinking game), proved the turning point for the company, which has thrived ever since. After 2003, Firebox successfully moved into the mail order, corporate and wholesale sectors. The website attracted nearly 16 million visits in 2011, and revenues had grown to £11m by 2008.

Acton Smith, however, spends the vast majority of his time today on Mind Candy, and has largely left Firebox to grow in the capable hands of Boardman and its managing directors. Mind Candy was formed in 2004 when Acton Smith, with the help of an early Firebox investor, secured $10m from venture capitalists to fund the business's first big project: an alternative reality treasure hunt called Perplex City. It took 18 months and a large amount of money to build, but the result was a commercial failure. Creatively, however, the game was remarkable, and demonstrated the appetite for risk and the taste for innovation that would soon see Acton Smith hit the big time with Moshi Monsters. But by the time he ventured into the children's gaming sector he was viewing it as 'a last throw of the dice' as the company was fast running out of funds. It was a good throw.

Moshi Monsters is a thoroughly realised online world, one that sprung from Acton Smith's imagination, in which children can adopt a monster, personalise it and use it to solve puzzles to earn a currency, which in turn can be spent in a virtual shop. There's also a variety of social networking features, and the business has been described by the likes of *The Guardian* and TechCrunch as a Facebook for kids. Mind Candy has designed the online puzzles and activities to be educational as well as fun, thereby earning the all-important buy-in from parents.

It's from parents, of course, that the revenue comes. A subscription model of £5 a month has been successful, but perhaps even more important today is the merchandise surrounding the Moshi world. Working with licensees means a low-risk model for the business, and thanks to magazines, cards, toys and music, there were total gross retail sales to a value of over $100m across all Moshi Monsters products in 2011. There's even talk of an imminent film. And it's truly a global business, with roughly a third of users in the UK, a third in the US and a third across the rest of the world. The business also has 130 licensing partners worldwide and has a retail presence within the US, Australia and New Zealand, the Nordic countries, Benelux, Poland, Israel, Dubai and South Africa.

Unsurprisingly, Moshi Monsters isn't the only brand aiming to be the number one in children's entertainment. The main competition Acton

Smith faces is from none other than Disney, after it bought Club Penguin from its Canadian founders for around $350m (£220m) in 2006. The challenge the firm faces is keeping its fans loyal, but so far this has not been a problem: the *Moshi Monsters* magazine is the best-selling in its category in the UK, the debut album reached number four in the UK charts, and the first Moshi Nintendo DS title became the longest ever at number one in Nintendo DS chart history. Children can't get enough.

Luckily then, the company hasn't stopped innovating and developing. Apps and mobile games mean that Moshi Monsters will have a strong presence in new ways of accessing toys and games. There are signs, too, that Mind Candy will be launching new projects: in 2012 it acquired games studio Origami Blue to launch its new innovation centre, Candy Labs, in Brighton. The company says: 'Candy Labs will be an R&D studio that experiments with new ideas to spin up the next wave of groundbreaking entertainment for children. The ideas will be a mix of digital and non-digital entertainment. Some of the concepts will be acquired from third parties, but most will originate in-house.' If just one of those concepts is anywhere near as successful as Moshi Monsters, there will be no stopping Mind Candy.

In 2011, early stage technology investor Spark Ventures (which also invested in the early stages of Firebox) sold half its stake in Mind Candy for £3.1m in cash, representing a 15-fold return on its 2004 investment. This deal values Moshi Monsters at a cool £125m. Since then, however, speculation has put its value at closer to £250m, and rumours of an IPO are rife. Those cute little critters have certainly been kind to Acton Smith.

Toby Ash

Company: New Heights
Young Gun in: 2003 (Age: 34)
Frustrated at the predominance of flat-pack furniture on the high street when kitting out his pad, Toby Ash and co-founder Gareth Williams started up New Heights in 1999, with the help of £750,000 from private investors, in order to sell quality wooden furniture on the high street. By 2003 the duo had opened eight stores in the UK and were projecting a turnover of £10m for the current year. The company bought MFI's Sofa Workshop business for £1.8m in October 2006, but just two years later, the tough economic climate meant the business was put into administration.

Darren Epstein

Company: Cards Inc
Young Gun in: 2004 (Age: 33)
Inspired by a trip to the US, Epstein started Cards Inc in 1989. Through organic growth and several acquisitions, it had become a major retail force with a turnover of £19.9m by 2004. In December 2006, the business was acquired by Corgi International.

Chris Fung

Company: Crussh
Young Gun in: 2004 (Age: 31)
Australian Fung was poised to return home to set up a smoothie bar before meeting Crussh's founder James Liamont. Liamont convinced him to stay in London and run his chain instead - and it's proved a wise decision for both parties. Under Fung's guidance, Crussh had opened its ninth store by 2004, and had reached a turnover of £2.2m. He is still there as managing director today, and now has 25 stores in London.

Sophie Oliver

Company: Coco Ribbon
Young Gun in: 2004 (Age: 31)
Started in 2002 with co-founder Alison Chow, the London-based boutique Coco Ribbon proved so successful that Kylie Minogue made a personal visit to request that it stock her latest lingerie range. The brand became known for its high-end underwear, clothing and gifts, but economic conditions proved too tough and it ceased trading in 2009, when the partners went their separate ways. Alison Chow later relaunched it as an online and fashion business out of Sydney.

Tamara Hill-Norton

Company: Sweaty Betty
Young Gun in: 2005 (Age: 34)
A year of frenzied growth for Hill-Norton's Sweaty Betty saw it expand from five to 17 stores and double turnover to £9m by 2005. Started in 1998 after Hill-Norton, a former buyer for Knickerbox, recognised the lack of specialist sports and leisurewear shops for women, the company grew organically before refinancing early in 2004. Today, the brand is a household name, and consists of 30 stores, including concessions in Selfridges and Harrods. The business has also become a multichannel retailer, with a growing website, mobile site and catalogue business.

Timothy Maltin

Company: Hardy Amies
Young Gun in: 2005 (Age: 32)
Introduced to the late Sir Hardy Amies by his great-aunt, who modelled for the prestigious fashion house in the 1940s, former grave maintenance entrepreneur Maltin brokered a deal to buy the then ailing company for a mere £200,000 in 1997. He reversed it onto OFEX before taking it to AIM in 2005 with a market cap of £5m. After raising money for the company and overseeing a significant boost in turnover, Matlin left the company in 2006 and now heads up PR agency Matlin PR.

James Murray Wells

Company: Glasses Direct
Young Gun in: 2005 (Age: 22)
Murray Wells was just 22 when he became a Young Gun in 2005, but was already shaking the optical industry to its foundations. Confused by how a pair of glasses – 'essentially some wire and two pieces of glass' – could cost £250, Murray Wells exposed and broke the big opticians' hold on the market. Using the final instalment of his student loan, he started selling glasses over the internet in September 2004 and achieved a first year turnover of £1m. Glasses Direct has now become something of a household name, and has secured over £10m from investors. The turnover of the company is approximately £13m, and Murray Wells is now also chairman of Hearing Direct, which he founded in 2010.

Heidi Gosman

Company: Heidi Klein
Young Gun in: 2005 (Age: 33)
For Gosman and co-founder Penny Klein, not being able to buy a bikini, pair of sunglasses and leg wax under the same roof represented a rare gap in the female retail sector. Formerly retail analysts, they raised private equity funding and launched luxury one-stop holiday shop Heidi Klein in April 2002. By 2005, there were two in London and one in Saint-Tropez, each generating £1m in sales a year. Since then, the founders have focused on developing their brand, which now includes a children's range, and is sold in concessions in Liberty in London as well as in other department stores.

Nick Wood

Company: Fruitboost
Young Gun in: 2005 (Age: 27)
Nick Wood's and his brother's two north-west-based smoothie bars proved so successful in their first year of trading that competitors were spotted outside trying to steal their secrets. According to Wood, theirs is a simple recipe of fresh fruit drinks and great customer service modelled on the $1 billion US juice bar industry.

Simon Tate

Company: Kew Health and Beauty
Young Gun in: 2006 (Age: 29)
Fresh out of university, Tate was made managing director of family business Wallace Manufacturing Chemists after his father's death. Six years later he had increased sales 50% across 90 countries, and he created Kew Health and Beauty in 2004 with Dominic McVey.

Russell Taylor

Company: Grafton House
Young Gun in: 2006 (Age: 29)
Working for Gordon Ramsay can be a baptism of fire for anyone hoping to succeed in the restaurant industry, but Taylor survived the abrasive chef to launch Grafton House with Quentin Dawson in 2005.

Martin Hunt

Company: Hunt For It
Young Gun in: 2006 (Age: 16)
Taking on the might of eBay would appear to be daunting enough, let alone if you are just 16 years old. Hunt, however, had business acumen in his blood – his father, Rikki, was a prominent entrepreneur. Hunt charged a percentage of the sale fee only, with customers able to bid via their mobile phones. In 2006, Hunt For It claimed to be the fifth largest auction site in the world. The David and Goliath story didn't have a happy ending, however, and the company was eventually dissolved.

Jo Chalker

Company: X Bar
Young Gun in: 2006 (Age: 35)
A former chartered accountant, banker and headhunter, Chalker decided to take on the unenviable task of attracting demanding City drinkers with the launch of her champagne bars, called Dion. Having raised almost £1m for her first two bars, retaining three-quarters of the equity, in 2006 around 2,000 workers from central London were visiting Chalker's urban oases every week. Although the economic environment meant that the third bar, in Canary Wharf, closed in 2008 after only a year, the original two bars are still serving thirsty City workers.

Harjeet Johal

Company: Underfivepounds.com
Young Gun in: 2006 (Age: 26)
The explosion of online retail provided a number of niches and Johal exploited a relatively simple one – selling clothing priced £5 or under. Sourcing products from China and India, Johal launched an effective marketing push following the website's launch in 2004, fronted by *Coronation Street* actress Shobna Gulati. He went on to work as managing director of retail chain Clothing Direct and is now a business commentator.

Anthony Cook

Company: Mobile Fun
Young Gun in: 2006 (Age: 28)
Operating in a congested market, Mobile Fun, which was set up by Cook in 2000, benefited from the upsurge in online spending. The business was offering more than 5,000 mobile accessories and 100,000 downloads to consumers in 2006, and organic growth saw its turnover figure rise from £7m in 2005 to £10m in 2006. Today, Cook is chairman of the company, which now has a presence in 14 countries including France, Germany, the Netherlands, Spain, Italy and the US. It has plans to continue its rapid international expansion, with international sales already accounting for more than 30% of total orders.

Terry Hogan

Company: New-Car-Discount.com
Young Gun in: 2006 (Age: 35)
A car salesman by trade, Hogan realised that by buying in bulk to meet online orders, he could operate without traditional overheads. Since launching in 2002, he has capitalised web traffic alongside car sales through advertising and partnerships with, for example, the AA. His site was attracting 120,000 users a month by 2006, and turnover was expected to hit £24m. Sadly, the administrators were called in in 2008, although by this time Hogan had already co-founded motoring.co.uk, which is designed to help people looking for a new car.

Andrew Crawford

Company: The Book Depository
Young Gun in: 2007 (Age: 35)
Crawford started up with a mission – to make all books available to all. Three years later, by 2007, the company was one of the UK's 10 largest booksellers, had a turnover of £24m and was able to source and dispatch 1.7 million titles within 48 hours from its Gloucester distribution centre. The firm continued to grow after Crawford was named a 2007 Young Gun, and by 2010 it was turning over more than £100m and dispatching books to more than 100 countries. It attracted the attention of rival and

e-commerce behemoth Amazon, which acquired the Gloucester firm for an undisclosed sum in June 2011. Crawford remains at the company as CEO.

Raj Rana

Company: Itihaas
Young Gun in: 2007 (Age: 30)
Serial entrepreneur Raj Rana has proven himself to be an accomplished restaurateur. Itihaas boasts some of India's finest chefs and service staff, and its traditional tikka masala-free menu has been extremely well received. In 2007 the Birmingham-based business was expanding rapidly, catering for top hotels. Today it caters for hotels such as those within the QHotels group and the Grand Connaught Rooms hotel. It has also opened Itihaas Brasserie within Selfridges in Birmingham.

Michael Welch

Company: Black Circles
Young Gun in: 2007 (Age: 28)
Former tyre fitter Michael Welch set up his second business, Black Circles, in 2001 as a tyre reseller that was 40% cheaper than Kwik Fit. A franchise model was launched in 2006, giving independent garages access to Black Circles' systems and stock, and 300 franchisees were on board by 2007. The business was due to turn over £10m that year, and had raised £1m in angel finance for working capital. Today, shareholders include Sir Terry Leahy, and Black Circles has over 1,300 contracted tyre-fitting outlets – the largest network of fitting outlets in the UK.

Claire Lewis

Company: Truffle Shuffle
Young Gun in: 2007 (Age: 23)
Celebrities being snapped wearing your products is quite possibly the best PR a clothing range can ask for – particularly when the star is Jennifer Aniston and the magazine is *Heat*. A-list endorsement from the *Friends* star, Amy Winehouse and many others catapulted turnover of online retro clothing firm Truffle Shuffle, which was started with £10 in 2004, to £2m

in 2007. Co-founders Lewis and Pat Wood had also just launched a new music T-shirt site, SugarBullets.com. Since then, Truffle Shuffle has become one of the most successful independent clothing websites in the UK, and its brand and licensing arm sells products through high-street retailers.

Elliott Zissman

Companies: Totally Fitness
Young Gun in: 2007 (Age: 32)
Starting in 2002 as www.totallyfitness.co.uk, by 2007 Zissman had established six stores, his contracts included schools, hotel chains, BP and Harrods, and the business had rented fitness equipment to the likes of Robert De Niro, Julia Roberts and Andre Agassi.

Alexander Amosu

Companies: Amosu Luxury Phones, Mobscasino.tv, Mind of an Entrepreneur
Young Gun in: 2007 (Age: 32)
Serial entrepreneur, columnist, TV presenter and DJ Alexander Amosu sold his first business, £6m-turnover RnB Ringtones, in 2004. In 2007, Amosu Luxury Phones was rivalling Vertu in the luxury mobile phone market, with price tags for gold and diamond-encrusted handsets ranging from £5,000 to £1m, while gaining column inches for its customised BlackBerrys and iPhones. The company created the world's most expensive suit in 2009.

Holly Tucker

Company: Notonthehighstreet.com
Young Gun in: 2008 (Age: 31)
Only a small percentage of the independent retailers applying to have their products sold on Notonthehighstreet.com are successful. The fact that a visitor to the site can browse over 50,000 goods (ranging from personalised glasses cases to solid silver egg cups)

from over 3,000 retailers demonstrates the appeal of the business to sellers and buyers alike.

The site was conceived to give small designers access to a wider consumer base: founders Holly Tucker and Sophie Cornish were among the first to successfully give consumers an easy way of rejecting mass-produced items in favour of one-off products. Even today, the site is a distinctive proposition in an ecommerce market getting ever more crowded. Artisan, quirky, eye-catching gifts and homeware have attracted a loyal customer base that drove turnover to £15.1m in 2010.

When Holly Tucker was named a 2008 Young Gun, the business was only two years old and was projecting a £3.7m turnover, up from £100,000 in the business's very first year, driven by a 25% commission on each sale and a £500 membership fee payable by every retailer the sites worked with.

The co-founders had also completed a funding round with Spark Ventures in exchange for a third of the company, and a second with Venrex LP, which invested £1m in 2008.

The direction in which the two women have led the 100-strong company since then has only made it a more appealing prospect among investors; in 2010 Greylock Partners and Index Ventures led on a funding round worth £7.5m. Most recently, in 2012, Fidelity Partners led on a £10m round, in which Greylock Partners and Index Ventures also participated. This large capital injection will be used for 'growing the Notonthehighstreet.com brand and expanding our offering within the UK,' says Tucker. 'We will be looking to extend our offering internationally and transform the global gifting market. Marketing and technology will be the main uses of investment.'

It's not only investors and customers who have been won over by the rise of the retailer. The founding duo have focused on attracting talent, and in 2011, at a time when they decided to take the step from 'in the business' to 'on the business', three senior executives were hired directly from global giants Google, PayPal and Amazon in the roles of chief operating officer, chief marketing officer and director of international development. The aim was, as Tucker told *Growing Business*, to take steps 'towards our vision of turning Notonthehighstreet.com into a very well-known brand in the UK and abroad'.

With this becoming an ever more achievable aim, the founders put as the key reason for their success (during a time that has proved challenging, often fatally so, for many retailers) their focus on the customer – a priority that can sound almost trite in its blatancy, but when genuinely done well can be the difference between success and failure a thousand times over. 'Every single decision you make needs to have your customer at the heart of it,' clarifies Sophie Cornish, 'from the price point to customer service. This is important - from research right through to sales, you need to be engaged with your customer, and they need to be engaged with you.'

Every single decision you make needs to have your customer at the heart of it.

Like many entrepreneurs offering a product or service that has genuine appeal, the duo believe they have also benefited from consumers' more careful decision making when it comes to spending money - if they are spending £20 on a gift, it has to be £20 well spent on something thoughtful, personal and different. They also credit consumers' desire to support small businesses - the retailers the site partners with - as an important draw.

The focus for Notonthehighstreet.com now is worldwide. 'We still have many avenues to explore here in the UK,' says Tucker, '[but] we are looking to take our offering to other countries. We will continue to change the way the world shops for themselves and for gifts.' To this end, in 2012 the business launched a multi-currency functionality facility, allowing it to take payments in US and Australian dollars and euros alongside sterling.

The company has been much lauded in the years since Holly Tucker was part of the Young Guns class of 2008. In 2011 alone its accolades included places in *The Sunday Times* Virgin Fast Track 100, the Deloitte UK Technology Fast 50, the Webby Awards, and *The Telegraph* Tech Start-Up 100. However, although Tucker admits that maintaining a work/life balance has been a struggle (both founders had small children when the business was in its infancy), the enterprise has proved rewarding in more ways than one: 'We have so many fantastic case studies of seller partners who have achieved incredible results since joining the site. Knowing we have enabled partners to, for example, go on their first family holiday in years, or quit their full-time job so they can turn their passion into their career, is so rewarding.'

Sarah Curran

Company: my-wardrobe.com
Young Gun in: 2008 (Age: 35)
Founded in April 2006, by the time it was two years old, online retailer my-wardrobe.com had made its name with designer womenswear, offering second line brands, such as Farhi from Nicole Farhi, and Vivienne Westwood Anglomania, which positioned it between the exclusive Net-a-Porter and the high-street appeal of ASOS. It had received over £2m in angel investment and was expecting a £3.5m turnover. Since then, the business has grown into the premier global online destination for everyday luxury designer fashion. my-wardrobe.com offers a unique curated edit of over 200 of the world's leading contemporary designer brands, attracting over 1.6m visitors every month. With more than 100 employees, and offices in the UK, Australia, the Middle East and Scandinavia, international sales have seen triple-digit growth.

Mitesh Soma

Company: Chemist Direct
Young Gun in: 2008 (Age: 32)
Chemist Direct was less than one year old when Mitesh Soma was named a Young Gun in 2008, but it was already profitable and projecting a turnover of around £5m for his first full year. The company buys stock in bulk, sells nationally and offers discounted prices on products that include everything from toothpaste to anti-malarials. Customers can also call to speak to registered pharmacists who check every order. Today Chemist Direct is one of Europe's largest online chemists, with more than half a million customers, and numerous product ranges including mother-and-baby products, nursery equipment, pet food, grooming and healthcare products, electricals and household cleaning products.

Vincent McKevitt

Company: Tossed
Young Gun in: 2008 (Age: 29)
McKevitt has proved that, with the right offering and know-how, you can thrive in even the most crowded of markets. Launched in 2005, Tossed

serves uber-healthy salads and by 2008 employed more than 70 staff across five London sites. That number has now risen to 10, including stores at both of London's Westfield Centres.

Fiona McLean and Clare Thommen

Company: Boudiche
Young Gun in: 2008 (Ages: 32 and 29)
Despite having little experience in retail, McLean and Thommen weren't afraid to question the received wisdom of the high street with the Edinburgh-based lingerie boutique they established in 2005. The two ex-accountants focus on personal service and creating a memorable customer experience, with lingerie chosen personally by the founders and sold by a team of trained bra fitters. An online boutique was launched in 2006 and a second store opened in Glasgow in 2008. Sadly, however, the business wasn't able to secure the investment needed to continue, and it went into administration in 2010.

Jimmy Metta

Company: Vanquish Wine
Young Gun in: 2009 (Age: 29)
Vanquish Wine was born in 2005, when former analyst Jimmy Metta found himself clearing a relative's wine cellar. He decided to sell the collection of Bordeaux vintages that he discovered. By the time he was named a Young Gun in 2009, Metta was regularly attending auction houses to buy fine wines with old friend and Vanquish co-founder David Elghanayan. Today the company claims to be London's leading luxury drinks specialist, selling to the UK on-trade, international institutions and private clients. In 2010, the firm launched its own wine investment vehicle; in 2011 it launched its managed personal wine portfolio, a bespoke product to create fine wine investment portfolios for private investors and institutions. And in 2012, it formed a partnership with Spectrum Wine Auctions, which is aiming for an ambitious revival of the London fine wine auction scene.

Dan Houghton and Eric Partaker

Company: Chilango
Young Gun in: 2010 (Ages: 33 and 35)
Entrepreneurs Eric Partaker and Dan Houghton are confident that 'Chilango is a global brand in the making' and it's hard not to agree. The business was launched in 2007 with £4.5m from external investors providing the catalyst, and today comprises three Mexican fast-casual restaurants. In 2009 it had just won two Zagat awards for the No. 1 Mexican Restaurant in London and the No. 1 Best Buy - another important step on the way to fulfilling the founders' aim of Chilango becoming a national chain in just a few years.

Kevin Flood and Mike Harty

Company: Shopow
Young Gun in: 2011 (Ages: 22 and 23)
Kevin Flood and Mike Harty were straight out of university when they started Shopow, but didn't let this stop them raising £380,000 from investors to develop software, and £500,000 to fund the launch and marketing. Angels were won over by the concept, which is a 'social shopping engine and community', in which users can compare prices from thousands of stores, find reviews and rate and comment on stores.

Since its launch in May 2010, the business had already achieved revenues of over £3m by the time the pair were named 2011 Young Guns. Co-founder Flood says the main challenge so far has been 'educating traditional bricks-and-mortar retailers about the advantages of engaging socially and using multichannel services to grow their sales'. However, the pair are confident that the business can achieve a 'critical mass' in the UK, and the entrepreneurs are looking to expand into the USA and mainland Europe imminently.

Emily Bendell

Company: BlueBella
Young Gun in: 2011 (Age: 30)
Described by founder Emily Bendell as specialising in 'sensual products aimed at the *Sex and the City* generation', BlueBella is carving its own

niche as a luxurious but affordable lingerie and 'love stuff' specialist. The company distinguishes itself from its competitors through its network of 'social sellers'; as well as selling its range of lingerie and products online, Bendell has modernised the 'party plan' sales model, giving hundreds of women the chance to earn money as BlueBella consultants.

Despite the fact that some people are uncomfortable with the business's raison d'être (including a certain Ann Widdecombe, who declined to present Bendell with a business award she had won), BlueBella has received over £200,000 from private investors, as well as £50,000 from female angel group Addidi. Bendell is now focusing on growing the UK network of party planners, with the aim of exploring new sales routes and other territories in the long term.

Mark Pearson

Company: MyVoucherCodes
Young Gun in: 2011 (Age: 31)
By the time he was 31, Mark Pearson had achieved more than most entrepreneurs manage in a lifetime. The former chef has created Britain's biggest voucher and deals network, and has established an extraordinarily successful business model. His business, MyVoucherCodes, was achieving profit margins of more than 90% on £10m turnover by 2011, a figure that was forecast to grow to £12m in 2012. The firm is now partnered with over 3,500 retailers (including Amazon, Tesco and Dixons) across 12 countries and MyVoucherCodes was valued at £60m by *The Sunday Times* Rich List.

To cap it all, Pearson has managed to fund every penny of expenditure himself, and thus kept 100% of the equity. Unsurprisingly, he is now earning widespread renown, having been a *Secret Millionaire* on Channel 4 and recognised at the Ernst & Young Entrepreneur of the Year awards, in addition to Young Guns. His firm was also identified as one of the UK's fastest growing companies in 2012 when it was listed in *The Sunday Times* Tech Track 100 league.

However, not content with the success of MyVoucherCodes, Pearson launched design-orientated website HushHush.com in 2012, which promises users significant savings on fashion, interiors, food and drink. The launch collection included the likes of Calvin Klein, Dolce & Gabbana and French Connection, and Pearson set up the business with a £1m budget and no external funding.

George Graham and Henry Graham

Company: Wolf & Badger
Young Gun in: 2012 (Ages: 26 and 31)
Brothers George and Henry Graham opened their first boutique, in trendy Notting Hill, in February 2010. Within a matter of months it had been named one of Britain's best boutiques by *Vogue* and picked by *Time Out* as the sixth best shop in London. The stir it caused in the retail world was due to its unique offering. The business provides fully serviced retail space to new, carefully chosen designers for a month or more - all for the same price as a weekend stall at London's Portobello Market. Wolf & Badger receives 10% of sales and also offers retail and merchandising consultancy services to supplement its revenues. A syndicate of angel investors has put £800,000 into the venture, and the brothers expect to see a turnover of over £1m in 2013. New stores have recently been opened in Porto Montenegro and London's Mayfair.

Telecommunications

James Murray

Company: Alternative Networks
Young Gun in: 2004 (Age: 34)

If James Murray could have taken a peek into a crystal ball when he was a 2004 Young Gun, we have no doubt it would have been a gratifying glimpse into the future. At that stage, Alternative Networks was on a very promising trajectory. The telecoms provider was 10 years old and had 10 years of sustained growth and profitability under its belt. In 2005 it saw sales of £45m, up from £32.5m in 2004. All growth had been entirely organic, funded through cashflow, with no debt taken on at all. Fast-forward seven years, and the business posted a turnover of £117m in 2011, a year that also saw acquisitions, its highest profits, and Murray being named as one of the 50 most influential leaders in the UK mobile industry.

Murray has grown Alternative Networks into one of the UK's leading telecommunications providers. It works with world-leading brands including BT, O2, Vodafone, Mitel and Avaya and supplies the telecommunication solutions to more than 5,000 SME and small corporate firms. The firm now employs 500 staff, based in six locations throughout the UK.

The key turning point in the acceleration of the company's expansion came in 2005, a year in which the business produced a pre-tax profit of £3.9m and in which Murray picked up the prestigious Ernst & Young Entrepreneur of the Year award. Fuelled by the desire to pursue a strategy based in no small part on acquisitive growth, Murray decided to take the business to junior stock market AIM. The decision, never taken lightly by owner-managers, proved a wise one. Since then, Murray has prioritised growing organically, with the occasional catalyst of a carefully chosen acquisition. He has focused, sensibly, on resisting the temptation to rush into such acquisitions, believing that each one needs to be thoroughly integrated and cross-selling opportunities maximised to allow as much organic growth as possible.

Certainly, investors have been convinced by the direction in which he has taken the firm over the last few years. Murray has steered Alternative Networks through a recession and through a tough time for the industry, and Alternative has remained a popular investment option. In 2011 the company was named in *Investors Chronicle*'s Top Five 'Steady Winners' feature, and analysts have credited the business's progressive dividend policy as one that sets it apart from other fast-growing telecoms businesses.

Financially, 2011 was a strong year for the firm, in which it saw its highest recorded sales, adjusted profits, operating cash receipts and dividends. Revenues increased 22% to £117.3m, and the 2010 acquisition of computer network integrator Scalable for £7.5m (with an extra £2.5m payable on growth targets being reached) had seen results, with Scalable posting healthy profits. Half-yearly results for 2012 were also positive, with a profit increase of 33% on the same period the previous year (to £5.59m), despite a slight drop in turnover. Alternative also announced a 9% rise in its mobile subscriber base. Murray described the market conditions as 'challenging', but said: 'The major components of our growth strategy all played their part. We continued to increase our market share; we maintained high levels of cross-selling across our customer base and saw reduced churn; and we invested in areas where we already know we have a competitive advantage.'

His firm continues to give something of a masterclass in growth strategies and he is open to making further acquisitions that bring additional commercial opportunities, add value and make the firm even stronger. Organic growth will focus on larger clients, while keeping churn low and improving processes and services.

James Murray was only 24 when he founded Alternative Networks. He was dyslexic and left school at 16 with very few O levels. Having worked for a telecoms company, he rose to become its top salesperson before he decided to launch Alternative Networks using a £10,000 loan plus £4,500 of his and his co-founder's own savings. Where his journey with Alternative Networks will end is anyone's guess - it surely has become an attractive acquisitive target itself - but presiding over a company he built up from nothing to one with a market cap of £142m makes Murray one of the most impressive UK entrepreneurs you're likely never to have heard of.

Richard Stubbs

Company: UK Explorer
Young Gun in: 2004 (Age: 34)
Started with Martin Hickman in 1998, Stubbs developed UK Explorer into a leading supplier of internet connection solutions to hotels and airports. Turnover in 2004 was expected to grow by a minimum of 80% from £747,000 in 2003. The firm was sold in 2005.

Andrew Pearce

Company: Powwownow
Young Gun in: 2005 (Age: 32)
Having started call centre company Inkfish, which was sold for £12m with him taking a seat on its FTSE 400 board, by 2005 Pearce was doing it all again. This time, with co-founder Paul Lees, Pearce started applying the easyJet logic to voice conferencing, offering low-cost calls without bridging fees or registration. When he was named a Young Gun, Powwownow was operating in seven European countries, and was expecting to see turnover grow from £1.25m to £6m in 2006. Today, Powwownow is Europe's fastest growing free conference call provider and operates in 15 countries. Pearce is CEO of holding company Via-Vox, which alongside Powwownow also comprises allconferencecalls and all-call, plus web-conferencing brand Yuuguu. The 2011 turnover of Via-Vox reached £7m.

Justin Hamilton-Martin

Company: 8el
Young Gun in: 2005 (Age: 33)
As a salesman in the telecoms sector in the late 1990s, Hamilton-Martin sensed growing dissatisfaction at the inflexibility of large wholesalers. With co-founders John Rees and Martin Gray, he launched 8el in 1999 to take on the big boys, winning corporate contracts by offering flexible payment solutions and better support. In 2005, 8el could boast a £6m turnover and more than 35,000 users. As managing director, Hamilton-Martin has been instrumental in transforming the company into a leader within the networking and VoIP marketplace in the UK.

Nick Claxson

Company: Comtec Enterprises
Young Gun in: 2007 (Age: 30)
When Nick Claxson was named a 2007 Young Gun, his ICT solutions business was turning over more than £6m and specialised in enabling secure, converged IP communications. The firm was also gearing up for its third acquisition. Today, Comtec is part of the eponymous Claxson Group, which is made up primarily of complementary technology companies. These include DP Direct, one of the largest direct mailing houses in the south of England; Sargasso Networks, a hosting company based in the US; Latitude UK, an IT support and maintenance service provider; IP Cameras; and Comtec Media, a website design, development and hosting company.

Stewart Yates

Company: TFM Networks
Young Gun in: 2007 (Age: 35)
Family-run business TFM Networks was born in January 2004. A virtual network operator, the company buys network services from a number of suppliers such as BT, and re-wraps them for clients including H&M, Travelodge and Yotel, offering average cost savings of around 40%. One of the biggest challenges, Yates says, has been building corporate-grade systems in a small business environment. However, the business excels in areas that are often poorly implemented by the company's competitors, such as billing, Yates says. Today he is looking to acquisitive growth to drive the company forward, and he completed the acquisition of Conexion Communications in 2012.

Jo Groves

Company: Active Digital
Young Gun in: 2007 (Age: 29)
Jo Groves and brother Richard created business mobile and data solutions provider Active Digital when she was just 16 and he was 20 - with him giving up his England Boys golf career to pursue it. By 2007, Active was working with all the major mobile providers, had grown organically for 12 years and was turning over £5.6m. Its tailored communications packages promise to boost productivity and cut clients' costs. By constantly

evolving in line with the telecommunications industry, Active Digital claims to be a leader in the business mobile industry, working as one of the top O2 partners in the UK.

Matthew Riley

Company: Daisy Communications
Young Gun in: 2007 (Age: 33)
When Matthew Riley was named a Young Gun of 2007, he was not short of ambition for his company, Daisy Communications. It was already shaping up to be a small jewel in the UK telecoms scene, posting a turnover of £23.6m at only six years old. Riley, however, was expecting big things, projecting a £100m turnover by 2010. It's safe to say that this target was well and truly smashed. His company, now Daisy Group, posted £348.6m revenues in 2012.

Founded as a one-stop provider of communications, for the first five years Daisy Communications grew rapidly, solidly and entirely organically. Riley held 100% equity in 2007, and, as the service provider to 20,000 SMEs, the business was starting to make good on its promise to become a serious threat to BT. There were signs, too, of the imminent and now-famous acquisition trail: 15 acquisitions had already taken place, all of which were completed without the need for any external capital. At this stage, bank debt was financing acquisitive growth, but it wasn't too long before the scale of the company's ambition, namely in terms of consolidation, required an extra boost of funding.

In 2009, Riley took the Lancashire firm to junior stock market AIM. The business backed into Freedom4 Group, previously known as Pipex, and the entire group was rebranded as Daisy Group. Riley was left with around 25% of the business, and took out approximately £30m in cash. The IPO raised £83m, and the turnover of £53m grew to more than £100m.

The IPO meant that Daisy was free to pursue consolidation aggressively. By October 2012, the group had completed around 39 acquisitions. The group's strategy for consolidating the fragmented communications market has been at the heart of the company's success, and economic conditions have played into Riley's hands by making it possible to buy at competitive prices.

Targeted acquisitions were then, and are now, seen by the company as strategically important, not only to increase the customer base and expand the product portfolio, but through opportunities to cross-sell and up-sell to customers.

However, this is not to say that organic growth has completely taken a back seat. In fact, today the rate of acquisitive growth has slowed, with only two companies bought in the financial year 2011–12. One reason for this is the focus the company places on integration. Daisy believes that its track record in quickly integrating acquisitions has helped distinguish it from other communications industry consolidators, and 2011–12 was a year in which this integration was a priority. So although further acquisitions from Daisy Group are on the cards, the furious pace of consolidation has already started to relax.

It's too difficult for large companies to have that personal service. Our salesmen actually go to every customer to discuss their options.

The company first made a name for itself among existing and potential customers through its unwavering focus on customer service. Back in 2007, Riley was aware that the company's minnow-like nimbleness helped it achieve this, telling *Growing Business*: 'It's just too difficult for a company as large as BT to have that personal service. Our salesmen actually go to every customer to discuss their options.' With an eye on the future, though, he admitted: 'As we grow, it will get more difficult for us to keep that personal element, too.' It's a challenge Riley and the Daisy Group seem to have overcome. In the 2011–12 financial year, revenue grew by 31%, from £266.3m to £348.6m, and adjusted EBITDA (earnings before interest, taxes, depreciation and amortisation) increased from £40.7m to £56.3m, an uplift of 38%. All this from a company Riley started in his garage.

The overall ambition for Daisy is to create one of the largest UK providers of telecommunications services and solutions to the SME and middle market. The steps Riley has taken towards this aim have already attracted the attention of Lord Sugar. In 2011, Riley made his first appearance on *The Apprentice*, grilling contestants in the final of the series. He then resumed his role as trusted lieutenant to Sugar in the 2012 series. If any business deserves to be recognised on prime-time television for its consistent and rather spectacular success, Daisy is surely it.

Jonathon Burrows

Company: Ask4
Young Gun in: 2008 (Age: 26)
Burrows launched Ask4, which supplies telecoms services to multiple-tenanted buildings, such as student halls of residence and apartment blocks, in 2000, when he was just 18. This followed three and a half years spent building Ask4's own infrastructure to deliver these services, funded by £750,000 of angel investment. By 2008, the business had been doubling in size, profitably, for the previous three years and had reached a turnover of £2.5m. In 2009, it launched a business services subsidiary and it is now on target to deliver turnover of over £10m, with profits of £1.5m.

Rob Booth

Company: In Call Solutions
Young Gun in: 2011 (Age: 35)
Despite being formed in only 2006, call-handling provider In Call Solutions is in the enviable position of having a predicted 2012 turnover of over £6m, and having been profitable since day one. Although it supplies exclusively to the UK telecoms reseller market, through its resellers, it currently supplies around 15,000 end-user business customers, which include high-street retailers, banks, sports-related companies, public sector organisations and media firms. Founder Rob Booth has his eye on the long term, saying 'the aim is to become the leading specialist supplier of numbers and inbound call handling in the UK - a £100m turnover business by 2015 - and look at all options for the business at that stage'. Organic growth has been strong so far, but to reach the 2015 target Booth is hoping to secure funding to allow the company to begin a new strategy of acquisition alongside product diversification.

Chris Harrison

Company: Collstream
Young Gun in: 2012 (Age: 33)
Self-taught IT developer and technical design expert Chris Harrison co-founded Collstream in 2005, aged 26. Since then, the Derby-based business has grown into a leading provider of SMS, voice messaging and

interactive voice response (IVR) solutions to clients including utility companies, Premier League football clubs and retail stores. Due to Harrison's and co-founder Ian Maxfield's decision to eschew external investment, the business has remained debt-free since day one. This makes its 2012 turnover of £3m, and its 50% year-on-year growth, arguably even more impressive. Harrison is now predicting continued strong growth and expansion into new markets as the use of mobile technology and SMS continues to increase. The company is achieving widespread recognition, having ranked at number 150 on the Deloitte Technology Fast 500 EMEA 2012, a ranking of the 500 fastest growing technology companies in Europe, the Middle East and Africa. Collstream grew revenues by an impressive 951% during this period.

Tom O'Hagan

Company: Virtual1
Young Gun in: 2012 (Age: 35)
Founded in 2007, network operator Virtual1 has made a name for itself in a crowded marketplace. Delivering connectivity and cloud solutions exclusively to the wholesale market, the business is predicted to grow organically to £20m by 2014. The company has more than 200 wholesale customers and installs and manages wide area networks (WANs) on behalf of its partners, which range from SMEs to major international corporations. Tom O'Hagan himself is something of an expert when it comes to the telecommunications industry, having worked in the sector for more than 12 years, and his business now employs over 30 people. The company's rapid growth led to it being named by the Deloitte Technology Fast 50 as the fastest growing telecommunications firm in the UK in 2012, and the fifth fastest growing company in the UK overall.

Wholesaling

Shelim Hussain

Company: Eurofoods
Young Gun in: 2003 (Age: 30)
In 2003, eight years after launch, Shelim Hussain's business was turning over £37m, had offices in the US and UK, and was employing 300 people. Not bad for his first job after his A levels. This impressive trajectory continued with some style, and today Eurofoods employs 1,500 people worldwide, has a turnover of over £70m and has become the UK's largest supplier to the Asian food market.

Richard Freedman

Company: ACS Clothing
Young Gun in: 2004 (Age: 32)
By 2004, Freedman had grown ACS Clothing into the world's largest supplier of kilts, with a turnover of £2.5m. In 2006 it expanded into formal wear, and the firm, which Freedman co-founded with his father in 1997, is now Europe's largest formal hire business, providing a fully managed formal hire service to around 1,500 retail stores. In 2011, ACS Clothing bought its main competitor, Etiquette Formal Hire.

Amy Farren

Company: MOMA Foods
Young Gun in: 2007 (Age: 27)
A year after launch, in 2007 MOMA was selling healthy oat-based breakfast products at five busy London railway stations. Amy and partner Tom Mercer had just taken out a loan through the Small Firms Loan Guarantee Scheme, to ramp up production to meet the rapidly expanding wholesale division. MOMA products had also started to be sold at Selfridges and were proving a huge hit in office cafes. Farren remained with the company for two years, but today MOMA Foods is run solely by Mercer.

Jack Ostrowski

Company: Yellow Octopus
Young Gun in: 2009 (Age: 33)
Jack Ostrowski came to the UK as a Polish immigrant and within three and a half years had established a multimillion-pound global business. His business, Yellow Octopus, exports outlet clothing from UK retailers, imports and distributes branded fast-moving consumer goods (FMCG), and also specialises in brand management in the value fashion sector. In 2010, Ostrowski was given the Queen's Award for Enterprise.

Dan Shrimpton

Company: Peppersmith
Young Gun in: 2012 (Age: 34)
Confectionery isn't an easy market to break into. But despite the dominance of conglomerates in the area, Dan Shrimpton and co-founder Mike Stevens have launched a range of mints, gum and sweets that differentiate themselves by being made from natural ingredients and by being the healthiest option on the market. The mints and gum are even accredited by the British Dental Health Foundation, as they help reduce the risk of plaque and tooth decay. The co-founders were two of Innocent Drinks' earliest staff, which may explain their bravery in the face of huge competition, and they have managed to get their products into around 2,000 stockists. They have also started their international expansion, trading in the Netherlands and Australia already.

Callum Bush

Company: MediaDevil
Young Gun in: 2012 (Age: 26)
MediaDevil, which designs and produces mobile phone accessories, is providing quality that can speak for itself. When founder Callum Bush bought an iPhone screen protector, only to be incredibly underwhelmed, he decided - in time-honoured entrepreneurial fashion - that he could do it better himself. So he did, and his screen protectors and touchscreen styluses are currently the best selling and most positively reviewed on Amazon UK and Amazon Italy. An unwavering focus on customer service

has paid dividends, and the company had the fourth most five-star-rated product on Amazon last year (sandwiched between Amazon's own Kindles and Adele's album *21*). The company was also presented with UK Trade & Investment's (UKTI's) Business Innovation Award in 2011, and visited 10 Downing Street after a recent win at the UKTI's inaugural Start-up Games.

Media and marketing

Richard Cobbold

Company: Digital View
Young Gun in: 2003 (Age: 34)
Digital View, co-founded by 2003 Young Gun Richard Cobbold, supplies the likes of Heathrow Express, Camelot and Boeing with flat-screen display units. The company has opened offices in the US and Hong Kong, as well as retaining a presence in the UK.

Emily Bliss

Company: The Brave Film Company
Young Gun in: 2003 (Age: 35)
Established in 1995 with a £60,000 loan by Bliss and Michelle Stapleton, The Brave Film Company had made its name as one of the top commercials production companies by 2003. Mercedes Benz, Ford, Peugeot, Cadbury, Mars, Hugo Boss, Royal Mail, Budweiser, Egg, the National Lottery and P&O Ferries had all seen the benefit of using the company's stable of directors. In 2006 the company was renamed Home.corp and makes content for every platform - TV, online, music video and documentary - in both the UK and the US.

Damian Cox

Company: EK Straas
Young Gun in: 2003 (Age: 28)
In 2003 Cox had already turned his outdoor advertising business EK Straas into one of the most talked-about new brands in the sector. Soon after being part of the inaugural Young Guns, he and co-founder Ben Goor sold the business to advertising giant Clear Channel. Having served an

earn-out, Cox started Ocean Outdoor in 2004, which has grown to post revenues of more than £17m in 2011, following an investment of £5.7m from Smedvig Capital two years earlier. Cox himself left the board in 2010 to pursue other business interests, which included starting outdoor advertising consultancy Wildstone in 2011. Meanwhile, Ocean Outdoor was bought by management for £35m in 2012.

Angus MacKinnon

Company: Nowwashyourhands
Young Gun in: 2004 (Age: 30)
After running his own graphic design studio and enjoying success as a director with design company Blueberry, MacKinnon teamed up with co-founders Neil Jeffries and Tim Spear to launch Nowwashyourhands in 2001. By 2003, the business had developed an impressive portfolio of clients including the BBC, Manchester United and Tesco and was named in *New Media Age*'s list of Respected Design Agencies 2003. The agency continued to thrive and build a strong reputation, before merging with Cleara to form Playgroup.

Liz Jackson

Company: Great Guns Marketing
Young Gun in: 2004 (Age: 31)
Founded in 1997, the same year as Jackson lost her sight, by 2004 the marketing firm's turnover was around £2m, and it had seven branches nationwide. Jackson has since been awarded an MBE for services to business in 2007, and even took part in Channel 4's *The Secret Millionaire*.

David Williams

Company: Avanti Screenmedia
Young Gun in: 2004 (Age: 35)
When Williams was named a Young Gun in 2004, Avanti was eight years old. In that time, former investment banker Williams had combined bank loans and angel finance with venture capital, ultimately listing on AIM. In

total, the company had raised £5m and grown its previous year's turnover of £1.4m to £4.6m in 2004. The 65-person set-up was also doubling profits year on year by placing screens in pubs, bars and high-street retailers, and made £564,000 from a £2.6m turnover in the nine months to December 2003, following the acquisition of competitor Translucis.

Claire Page

Company: Whitewater
Young Gun in: 2004 (Age: 34)
Page joined Whitewater in 1996 and along with her husband, Steven, led a management buyout in 1998. She went on to oversee Whitewater's introduction of a number of innovative products and methods that revolutionised the traditional fundraising model. The company won the Direct Marketing Association's UK award for innovation in 2004.

Paul Ephremsen

Company: Ideal Promotions
Young Gun in: 2004 (Age: 34)
Ephremsen co-founded Ideal Promotions with Paul Soames immediately after graduating in 1993, with just £2,000. By 2004, their ability to produce campaigns that 'locate consumers and engage them in branded conversations' had raked in £8.5m and created a workforce of 50 people. Since rebranded as iD Experiential, the company, of which Ephremsen remains CEO, is turning over around £12m, and is a leading UK experiential marketing company.

Al Gosling

Company: Extreme Group
Young Gun in: 2004 (Age: 33)
Gosling started the business in 1995, while still in his early 20s, selling extreme sports-based programmes to broadcasters. He then launched the Extreme Sports channel in a $20m joint venture with the programming arm of cable operator UPC and secured £2.7m in backing from highly successful entrepreneurs and serial investors Nigel Wray (Domino's Pizza)

and Chris Akers (Sports Internet Group). By 2004, the channel sat at the centre of a range of brands, including Extreme Drinks, Clothing and Retail and was turning over £24m. Since then Gosling has developed Extreme into a pioneering brand management and licensing company.

Seb Bishop

Company: Espotting Media
Young Gun in: 2004 (Age: 30)
2004 was an excellent year for Bishop's Espotting. A 67% increase in turnover and the company's first profitable quarter were followed by the merger with American NASDAQ-listed firm FindWhat.com in July. The company had become the largest independent paid-for listings provider, valued at around $180m. It was operating across three continents, had relationships with more than 100,000 online businesses and accounted for just under half of online marketing spend in the UK - some £150m. Bishop went on to become international CEO of (RED), the organisation created by Bono and Bobby Shriver to raise money for The Global Fund to fight HIV/AIDS in sub-Saharan Africa. And today he is the CEO of Gwyneth Paltrow's lifestyle company Goop.

Simon Franks

Company: Redbus
Young Gun in: 2004 (Age: 33)
Former City trader Franks started Redbus in his spare bedroom, with a film distribution business. Six years on, in 2004 that business had become one of the largest distributors in Europe and the fastest growing UK company (with a turnover of $50m), but film distribution was just one of the business's arms. Also under the Redbus banner were outdoor advertising, online media and production companies - all of which were profitable - with the latter responsible for *Bend It Like Beckham*. Today, Redbus is a UK-based acquisition vehicle, which seeks to acquire small businesses or business assets that require restructuring or refinancing, and return them to profitability. Franks remains with the business as chairman and largest single shareholder.

Matthew Bayfield

Company: Tree
Young Gun in: 2004 (Age: 30)
Tree, started in 2001 by Bayfield and Steve Mattey and employing 11 people by 2004, combines market research with data analysis and had already worked with the likes of Skoda, BMW, Canon, Austin Reed and O2. It was predicting a £1.4m turnover for 2004, carving a niche as a market research house that shuns the traditional ABC1 demographic models. The firm was sold to marketing business Chime Communications for £2m in 2010.

Tim Clyde

Company: The Minimart
Young Gun in: 2005 (Age: 32)
Handling multimillion-pound accounts for advertising giants Leagas Delaney and M&C Saatchi taught Clyde and co-founder Ed Chilcott everything they didn't want their business to be. The Minimart uses its network of independent photographers, film editors and artists to build bespoke teams for each campaign. The Minimart produced 14 TV adverts in their first year and by 2005 turnover had topped £1m. Completely self-financed, the pair were planning to grow organically by staying small but growing their collective of partners. The agency is still going strong today, with a client list that includes the BBC, Rubicon, Rimmel and Maximuscle.

Sharon Richey

Company: LoewyBe
Young Gun in: 2005 (Age: 32)
A successful entrepreneur in her native South Africa, Richey launched LoewyBe in 2003. LoewyBe, which licensed its name from marketing giant Loewy Group, offered experiential marketing solutions to clients such as Pampers, and, by 2005, turnover of £2.8m was expected to grow to £4.2m. In 2007, the agency was rebranded as BEcause Brand Experience. Its clients today include L'Oréal, Innocent, P&G, Adidas and British Gas, and the business has offices in Moscow and Sydney.

Damian Bentley

Company: Snowball
Young Gun in: 2005 (Age: 32)
In 2005, Damian Bentley's direct marketing agency had recorded 300% or more growth in the two years since he and two others set it up. The nine-person London business's luxury brand clients included Alfred Dunhill, Bang & Olufsen, and home fitness specialist Technogym. Turnover already stood at £2.2m. Bentley owned 40% of the business and expected to exit within five years. In 2009 he realised this ambition and the business was acquired by Tangent.

Keith Jordan

Company: Adwalker
Young Gun in: 2005 (Age: 31)
Having worked in his family business and launched his own web design company, Jordan, along with Simon Crisp, came up with the Adwalker concept in 2002. After three years of R&D and trials, the company floated on OFEX and then, in 2005, AIM, where it was valued at £14m and raised £4m to start roll-out in its home country of Ireland, the UK, Hong Kong and North America. Sadly, however, the company failed to make a profit, and went into liquidation in 2009.

Oliver Bishop

Company: Steak Media
Young Gun in: 2006 (Age: 29)
Bishop worked alongside 2005 Young Gun and brother Seb at Espotting before founding his search engine marketing firm in 2005. By 2011, it had secured private equity investment, expanded to offices in London, New York and Melbourne, had 94 employees, and clients included Virgin Holidays, Debenhams and Comparethemarket.com. In June 2011, Steak was bought by Dentsu Network - the fifth largest marketing communications company in the world. Bishop remains with the company as CEO.

James Layfield

Company: The Lounge
Young Gun in: 2006 (Age: 32)

Layfield ran Richard Branson's D3 and realised that there was another way of understanding the youth market than, as he says, 'wearing swanky jeans and getting a trendy haircut'. Consequently, with Sarah Gill, he created The Lounge, an experiential marketing company for companies wanting to reach the 18–30 age group. With Virgin as his first client, it wasn't long before the likes of Microsoft and Samsung signed up, helping Layfield generate a £1.5m turnover. This has since grown to over £5m. While still managing director at The Lounge, Layfield also found time in 2010 to set up City work-hub business Central Working, which has recently opened several clubs in London.

Ben Grant

Company: Addirect
Young Gun in: 2006 (Age: 26)

Grant secured £2m of venture capital funding to finance his mirrored advertising venture and made a first-year turnover of £3m. By 2006, the product had been licensed globally and secured another round of funding, this time worth £3m.

Sean Fergusson

Company: Brandedmedia
Young Gun in: 2006 (Age: 34)

In less than three years, Fergusson's CD and DVD multimedia duplication house had become a dominant player in the fulfilment market, with an impressive array of clients. Brandedmedia stood out from the crowd by 'hand-holding' clients through the entire process of creating, packaging and storing media. Its turnover of £3.2m this year was set to hit £6m in 2007. Fergusson remains managing director of the business, and has also founded digital marketing agency Top of the Search.

Simon Mansell

Company: TBG Digital
Young Gun in: 2006 (Age: 27)
When your own line manager asks to be demoted rather than manage you, it's pretty obvious you should be your own boss. Mansell realised this and, despite establishing his digital marketing firm TBG during the dotcom crash in 2001, achieved 40% year-on-year growth by 2006, resulting in a £10m turnover. Crediting the capture of clients, such as American Express, to excellent in-house training, Mansell targeted companies needing clever direct marketing to great effect. The company now has offices in nine cities around the world, and in 2012 was accepted into the Facebook Preferred Marketing Developer (PMD) programme. That year it was also named in *The Sunday Times* Best 100 Small Companies to Work For list, which noted that the average age of the workforce is 28, with 60 of TBG's 67 employees under 35.

Hasfa Abubacker

Company: Pitch TV
Young Gun in: 2006 (Age: 32)
After helping to double margins while working as a buyer on a shopping channel, Abubacker saw the opportunity to improve on US infomercials. She launched her own channel, Pitch TV, in 2005, becoming the youngest person ever to do so in the sector. Having raised £2.5m through private investors, she bought channel space from the Express Group, after initially, she says, 'being laughed at – it's a very male-dominated industry'. Sadly, however, the enterprise didn't succeed and closed down in 2009.

Ben Allan

Company: The Insert & Leaflet Team (TILT)
Young Gun in: 2007 (Age: 31)
Big brands were proving very keen to advertise in TILT's recommended consumer guides in 2007, which covered areas such as insurance, loans and mortgages, motoring and money. TILT had started partnering with

experts such as celebrity chef Antony Worrall Thompson and money-management guru Alvin Hall, who provided tips on a sponsorship basis. Around 53 million guides were distributed in 2007. The company, however, has since been dissolved.

Rupert Loman

Company: Eurogamer
Young Gun in: 2008 (Age: 25)
Loman set up Eurogamer at 16 as a place for games fanatics to discuss and review the latest releases online. He soon realised the business potential of the site he had created with his brother. In bringing together a group of avid gamers, it was an advertiser's dream - and they soon flocked. Based in Brighton, by 2008, Eurogamer was being used by 2.4 million people every month and turning over £1.2m. Diversification into events has paid dividends and today the Eurogamer Expo is one of the biggest events in the gaming calender. As one of the world's leading games media businesses, the Eurogamer family of websites reaches more than 10 million unique users per month.

Satish Jayakumar and Michael Stephanblome

Company: AdJug
Young Gun in: 2008 (Ages: 29 and 35)
AdJug enables advertisers to buy space directly from website owners rather than through a network, giving them an unprecedented level of control over where their messages are displayed on the web and information about their return on investment. Having gained £1m funding from Benchmark Capital and 2004 Young Gun (and current CEO of Goop - the lifestyle company of Gwyneth Paltrow) Seb Bishop, AdJug received a further £3.3m from Balderton Capital and German media company Tomorrow Focus AG. In 2009, Tomorrow Focus increased its holding to 56%. Two years later, the company was acquired by Japanese advertising giant Dentsu, which in the same year also bought Steak Media, founded by fellow Young Gun Oliver Bishop.

Tim Drake

Company: Flipside Group
Young Gun in: 2008 (Age: 35)
Based in 16th-century barns rather than super-trendy offices, Flipside is proud to do things differently to your typical London agency. Comparatively speaking, Flipside employs smaller account-handling teams, or, as Drake puts it: 'We have 85% of people actually doing the work.' Clients include Toni & Guy, the United Nations, Anglo American and Dairy Crest, plus a number of smaller players, all attracted by the fact that the people they see at the pitch and speak to on the phone are the people doing the work.

Lyndon Nicholson and Dale Smith

Company: Article 10
Young Gun in: 2008 (Ages: 35 and 31)
Co-founders Nicholson and Smith launched their presentation design firm in 2004, and its turnover was set to reach £1.1m in 2008. The company's initial offering saw it providing everything from simple PowerPoint presentations to corporate videos for clients such as BP, Barclays and Unilever. When blue chips began to view Article 10 as a preferred supplier, Nicholson and Smith expanded its offering to cover online advertising, integrated marketing and event management; eventually they created five separate marketing agencies under the Article 10 umbrella. Nicholson exited via a management buyout in 2011 and went on to become head of leading content marketing agency Crowdbait.

Oli Norman

Company: DADA
Young Gun in: 2009 (Age: 31)
Set up in 2003, self-funded and profitable in its first few months, Glasgow-based DADA is a marketing agency with a difference. It enters joint ventures with its clients, which include Hilton and the BBC, often approaching them with unusual concepts. Founder Oli Norman also owns Sloans, Glasgow's oldest bar and restaurant, and itison, which has grown to become Scotland's leading daily deals site with more than a quarter of a million members.

Susanna Simpson

Company: Limelight Public Relations
Young Gun in: 2009 (Age: 31)
Public relations is a highly competitive industry, which unfortunately can sometimes be viewed as more of a hindrance than a help. However, in Limelight PR, founder Susanna Simpson has created an agency that is consistently described, refreshingly, as a joy to work with. Limelight's range of work covers both business-to-business and consumer campaigns. Headquartered in London, Limelight has offices in Dubai, Sydney and New York.

Claire Mason

Company: Man Bites Dog
Young Gun in: 2010 (Age: 35)
With more awards than any other business-to-business public relations consultancy in the UK, by 2009 Man Bites Dog had become bigger and better as a result of the recession, according to founder Claire Mason. She credits this to the fact that intelligent PR is becoming more business-critical than ever. Mason is concentrating on building on the firm's reputation and expanding its professional services client base. In 2012, the company was recognised in *PRWeek*'s Best Places to Work awards for the fourth year in a row.

Matt Connolly

Company: Enable Interactive
Young Gun in: 2010 (Age 33)
Enable Interactive found most of its early clients in the charity sector - building up a name for itself through work with organisations such as Greenpeace, Christian Aid and the British Red Cross. Despite this, the Bristol-based agency sadly closed its doors in September 2010. 'Unfortunately, with budgets under massive pressure in the not-for-profit sector, the climate is incredibly tough,' said the agency. Recently, Connolly embraced a change of direction, setting up myLovelyParent, a dating site that enables users to find dates for their 'older' parents. The site is

available in Australia, Canada, Ireland, New Zealand, South Africa, the UK and the US.

Sam Barnett

Company: Struq
Young Gun in: 2010 (Age: 27)
Sam Barnett started Struq at the height of the recession and, unable to get a loan or overdraft to fund the launch, set up the business on a debt of £2,000 that was owed to him. After some particularly perilous early days, Struq's client list soon grew to include a raft of household names, such as Ted Baker, French Connection, Swiftcover and John Lewis. At the same time, the company developed pioneering machine-learning technology that has changed the face of online display advertising. In 2012 the company raised $8.5m in a Series A funding round, which Barnett says will be used to fund overseas expansion.

Sam Conniff

Company: Livity
Young Gun in: 2010 (Age: 32)
'It's basically a marketing agency with a youth club in the middle,' says Sam Conniff, describing the controlled chaos that is the Livity workplace. The agency works with 12- to 21-year-olds to produce campaigns and content for clients including Google, the BBC, Channel 4, Sony, Adidas and the Cabinet Office, and simultaneously helps young people into education or employment. The business's client base has grown year on year, and over 1,000 young people work in the Livity offices each year, gaining practical, vocational experience.

The firm has been well recognised by external parties since Conniff was named a Young Gun and, along with co-founder Michelle Clothier, he was awarded the 2011 Ernst & Young Social Entrepreneur of the Year Award. 2012 saw Livity take home four awards at the MAA (Marketing Agencies Association) event, including Best Social Media Campaign, Best Consumer Campaign and Best of the Best for the Final Verse campaign developed for the NSPCC's ChildLine service. In 2013 the firm was shortlisted for four MAA Best Awards, which are hosted in partnership with the *Guardian*.

Justin Gayner, Wil Harris and Barney Worfolk-Smith

Company: ChannelFlip
Young Gun in: 2010 (Ages: 34, 28 and 35)
ChannelFlip makes content designed for online viewing, targeting men between 17 and 35, and its videos, featuring stars including David Mitchell and James Corden, had racked up over 35 million views by the time the founders were named Young Guns in 2010. The site aimed to deliver a premium environment for advertisers, and major clients included Cadbury, Volvo, O2 and the BBC. In 2012 the company was acquired by News Corp spin-off Shine Group, for an undisclosed sum.

Paul Thomas and Henry Braithwaite

Company: Market Makers
Young Gun in: 2011 (Ages: 29)
Few of the great business partnerships have been forged in a teenage band, but then Paul Thomas and Henry Braithwaite have always striven to be a little different. Their company, Market Makers, is set up to offer fresh solutions to common telesales and telemarketing problems, incorporating a host of value-added services such as target profiling.

Thomas and Braithwaite say their 'persistent focus is on taking a profession that historically has a bad reputation, and completely spinning it on its head', and this approach is reaping considerable rewards. Market Makers was set to turn over £7.2m in 2011, and the business has been named in *The Sunday Times* 100 Best Companies to Work For list four years in a row. The company has also funded charitable projects in Cameroon.

Warren Cowan

Company: Greenlight
Young Gun in: 2011 (Age: 34)
In 2001, when Warren Cowan founded specialist search and social marketing agency Greenlight, it was a struggle to convince potential clients that search engine optimisation (SEO) was something they had to start

taking seriously. Not a problem he faces anymore, and being ahead of the curve has led Greenlight to become the fastest growing and largest independently owned search and social marketing agency in Europe.

Cowan has managed to grow the business entirely organically, with a client list that includes names such as Santander, Sky, New Look and Thomas Cook, and 2011's £15m turnover was achieved without taking on any debt. An impressive focus on innovation means that Greenlight boasts a huge R&D department comprising mathematics PhDs, marketing experts and seasoned programmers, working hard to ensure that the agency is prepared for the ways in which the rapidly evolving digital marketing industry will develop.

James Robinson

Company: Zeffa
Young Gun in: 2011 (Age: 30)
Media agency Zeffa - which was only three years old when founder James Robinson was named a 2011 Young Gun - can count some high-profile names among its client list, a list that's growing all the time as the company demonstrates a 50% year-on-year growth. Robinson admits that securing clients wasn't easy: 'I really struggled with convincing potential clients that we were a credible alternative to their existing media agency. In times of economic uncertainty people stick with things they know and, more importantly, things that they trust.' However, realising that the key lay in reducing the risk for potential brands, as well as the cost, the business was able, in Robinson's words, to 'seize an opportunity as the new kid on the block'. He is now working on building a national network of offices, but doesn't believe in over-planning for the future. 'I find if you spend too much time planning you miss out on opportunities that present themselves. If you don't take up that opportunity, someone else will!' In late 2012, the agency was ranked at number 27 in the top 100 agencies outside London.

Jonathan Bramley

Company: In Your Space
Young Gun in: 2011 (Age: 35)
Even in times of plenty, you wouldn't put money on the success of a start-

up outdoor media agency. The industry is completely dominated by huge names, and even they have been struggling since recession struck, with giants such as Clear Channel feeling the pinch. Bramley, who founded In Your Space in 1999 at the tender age of 23, wasn't intimidated. His idea was to specialise in transport media for brands looking to target the modern mobile consumer, and with this focus he has won clients including Fox, BP and Sainsbury's. Furthermore, the company is focusing on international expansion, with offices in Australia proving successful. Bramley's different way of doing things is perhaps best exemplified by the fact that 20% of the company's profits go directly to charity, yet another way in which In Your Space stands apart from other players in its field.

Tom Morgan

Company: MVF Global
Young Gun in: 2011 (Age: 34)
MVF Global is built on strong foundations, according to co-founder Tom Morgan. The entrepreneur steered the lead generation start-up away from business he deemed risky, even if lucrative, and still got MVF Global on track to see a turnover of £8.5m in 2011. In addition, it has clients in over 30 different countries and has grown to over 50 staff.

Morgan says that 'the greatest part of the achievement for me is doing everything from a standing start with no external support or funding'. Sustained growth may be down to the business's strategy of targeting fast growing sectors, such as green energy, and strong economies, including Germany, Brazil and China. New sectors and territories are being assessed all the time. In 2012, the company ranked at number three in Startups.co.uk's Startup 100 list.

Emi Gal

Company: Brainient
Young Gun in: 2011 (Age: 25)
Emi Gal, at the tender age of 25, had already been involved in a number of start-ups, both in the UK and in his native Romania. Shoreditch-based Brainient is his latest, and makes video adverts more effective. It currently consists of three products: the first is a personalised video re-targeting platform, the second a solution that lets advertisers create interactive

video, and the third a DIY interactive video editor.

So far, Brainient has secured significant investment, including $800,000 from the Arts Alliance in 2010, and Gal says, with good reason, he's 'excited about the growth of the video advertising industry'. The company already has three offices, in London, New York and Bucharest.

James Connelly

Company: Fetch Media
Young Gun in: 2011 (Age: 25)
By the age of 25, Connelly was the co-founder of a mobile advertising agency that had campaigns running in 70 countries. Not only that: the business won clients including hotels.com, Paddy Power and Sony Music within a year, despite Connelly stating that getting clients to 'commit to decent investments into mobile' has been his biggest challenge. 'There is still a cautious approach to buying new media in times of economic uncertainty,' he notes. This isn't putting him off innovating, though, as he plans to continue to push preconceptions of what can be done with mobile marketing, while growing into global territories – a San Francisco office was opened recently.

Energy

Neil Tierney

Company: Onzo
Young Gun in: 2010 (Age: 32)
Of all the sectors to launch into, energy and water is probably one of the largest and most traditional. But this didn't deter Neil Tierney. He started Onzo in 2007 to provide utility companies with the tools to help consumers understand and manage their energy consumption. With some sizeable venture capital investment in 2008 smoothing the way, by 2010 the business could count Scottish and Southern Energy among its clients. Since then it has been expanding overseas and is now a global leader in big data and analytics for utilities. Tierney left the company in 2011 and now works to transform healthcare through various business ventures.

Stephen Fitzpatrick

Company: Ovo Energy
Young Gun in: 2010 (Age: 32)
By 2010, Ovo Energy was supplying gas and electricity to more than 30,000 homes across the UK. An impressive statistic, but, as Fitzpatrick points out, that translates to one in every 800 homes, meaning that there is plenty of room for growth. He has focused on employing bright young graduates and hopes to see his Cotswolds-based business, which buys wholesale energy and sells it on to customers, become a top 10 UK employer. An emphasis on greener energy also gives the business another way of standing out in a tough market. Today the business has amassed a customer base of more than 100,000.

Christopher Baker-Brian and Mansoor Mohammad Hamayun

Company: BBOXX
Young Gun in: 2011 (Ages: 24 and 22)
Solar energy supplier BBOXX certainly isn't short of ambition. It was formed by Christopher Baker-Brian, Mansoor Mohammad Hamayun and Laurent Van Houke as a for-profit spin-off from e.quinox, a charity at Imperial College London. The company develops methods of distributing renewable energy to developing countries. Its innovative portable solar products are aimed at people in developing countries who do not have access to electricity or who live in areas where the grid electricity is unstable. BBOXX works with local partners around the world who invest in the right to represent their products and brand in their respective markets. The company has already launched partnerships in Rwanda, the Democratic Republic of Congo, Pakistan, Iraq and Malawi.

BBOXX also reaches its customers through non-governmental organisations, governmental contracts or direct retail through its own distribution networks. As well as developing new products, BBOXX's founders are continuously in negotiations with potential future partners to open up new markets around the world, and the company is developing different franchising models to give people in developing countries the opportunity to start renewable energy businesses.

Leisure

Scott Lloyd

Company: Next Generation Group
Young Gun in: 2003 (Age: 28)
It hardly seems fair to mention that Scott is following in his father, David's, footsteps in the leisure industry. Scott has single-handedly raised £66m in private equity and £80m in debt for his new fitness clubs. His father is involved as chairman of the Next Generation Group, but Scott does things his own way. After a decade of growth, the company was acquired by the investment firm London & Regional Properties in 2006. In 2008, Whitbread sold the David Lloyd chain to London & Regional and HBOS for £925m. Scott is now chief executive of the enlarged chain, known as David Lloyd Leisure Group. The company runs 78 clubs in the UK and 10 in Europe, including locations in Belgium, the Netherlands, the Republic of Ireland and Spain.

Steve Lowy

Company: Umi Hotels
Young Gun in: 2011 (Age: 30)
Lowy set up his hotels business (which 'provides five-star service at three-star prices') in 2007 and by 2011 had seen turnover increase to over £4m from the three hotels in Brighton, London and Moscow. Being, as Lowy admits, a 'small fish in a big pond' hasn't deterred him, and, as the brand grows, Umi Hotels is starting to make its voice heard among the hotel industry giants, especially after *The Sunday Times* named one of his properties in its list of the top 50 budget hotels in the world. He is now considering implementing a franchise model in order to take the business further afield and build its presence in Europe, and would like one day to open a hotel school to inspire more young people to enter the industry.

Charity

Tim Campbell

Company: The Bright Ideas Trust
Young Gun in: 2008 (Age: 31)
Tim Campbell has come a long way since winning the first series of *The Apprentice*. In 2007, he left his six-figure-salary job at Amstrad to launch The Bright Ideas Trust, and it has proved to be a triumph. Supported by a range of corporate partners, the trust aims to unlock the entrepreneurial talent in Britain's young people, aged 16 to 30, by investing in their business ideas in return for an equity stake. Unlike other venture capital firms, any return goes back to the trust to help other young start-ups. Campbell was CEO of the charity until recently, and now divides his time between business interests, speaking engagements and his role as the Mayor of London's Ambassador for Training and Enterprise. In February 2012 he was awarded an MBE for his efforts to encourage enterprise.

Property

Shaid Luqman

Company: Pearl Holdings (Europe)
Young Gun in: 2004 (Age: 35)
In 2004, Shaid Luqman was riding high. When MPs, premiership football stars and prominent entrepreneurs wanted to build their property portfolios, they went to Luqman. The company, set up in 2000 and with bases in Manchester, London, Switzerland and Saudi Arabia, provided bridging finance in situations where banks would not be able to move fast enough. The pipeline of deals and finance to back clients' purchases came from the high-street banks, however, with £150m from a syndicate led by Barclays. Turnover to December 2004 was around £30m, and one high-street bank had offered £350m for the business. In 2006, Luqman's empire, since renamed Lexi Holdings, went into administration with debts of £100m amid allegations of dishonesty. Court breaches meant that Luqman himself served two jail terms.

Alex Michelin

Company: Finchatton
Young Gun in: 2005 (Age: 29)
Finchatton properties are statements of wealth: if Ferrari made apartments it would make them like Finchatton does. From bullet-proof glass to wireless networked sound systems, every property incorporates the latest technology and designs. Having worked in mergers and acquisitions for HSBC and a venture capital fund for start-ups, Michelin and co-founder Andrew Dunn raised £3m in private equity and started work on their first property in 2002. In 2005, turnover hit £15m with profits of 15% to 25% per property. The developer has now completed on over £870m of prime property in the last decade, with another £300m in the pipeline.

Gemma Bertenshaw

Company: Qdos Developments
Young Gun in: 2007 (Age: 29)
Having established an impressive rental and development portfolio, Bertenshaw teamed up with entrepreneur Howard Bilton, founder of the American Golf Discount chain, after they met through a mutual friend. In 2006 they formed luxury property brand Qdos. They bid successfully in a number of competitive land auctions and, as a result, their portfolio comprised eight prime sites in the north-west. Today, Bertenshaw works on her company gb Homes, which provides a full range of services including land acquisition, planning proposals, design and build and a full interior design service.

Steve Andrews

Company: SimpliGroup
Young Gun in: 2007 (Age: 29)
Steve Andrews co-owned finance and property company SimpliGroup with twins Rob and Chris Downham. What began as a financial services provider in the UK had morphed by 2007 into a diverse group of companies offering property development and financial and insurance services across Bulgaria and the UK. Its pièce de résistance was a 90,000 square metre environmentally aware 'well-being village' in Bulgaria. The development of 150 properties, spa centres and organic restaurants won a five-star award. Andrews left the company in 2009.

Robert Leigh

Company: Devono Property
Young Gun in: 2008 (Age: 29)
Devono is a commercial property company with a difference – it's the only one to exclusively represent tenants looking to rent office space in London. Offering unbiased advice, Devono helps tenants find the best office space for the best possible terms. Boasting an unrivalled level of market intelligence, in the last five years it has acquired more offices for businesses than any other property company in London. Customers range from start-ups to Toshiba, Bebo and E.ON.

Conclusion: Tips and advice from the Young Guns

The businesses in this book have proved that there is no one-size-fits-all recipe for success. The most exciting, innovative, fast growing and profitable businesses in the preceding pages have only the fact that they were started by an entrepreneur aged 35 or under in common. They span all sectors, growth strategies and ambitions.

Similarly, the young business people behind them are a varied flock. There can sometimes exist a preconception that to set up a successful business one needs a host of advantages: a wealthy background, an education that opens doors, contacts and people in high places willing to help. But that isn't true. Entrepreneurs come from all backgrounds, all sections of society, all ages. Some of this generation's most successful business people hold no qualifications (Sir Philip Green, for example, who left school at the age of 15), while others are highly educated. The fact is that successful entrepreneurs - of any age - create their own opportunities and advantages. Perhaps among the Young Guns, this is best exemplified by Duane Jackson, who grew up in a children's home, where he took the initiative to teach himself how to program computers. Expelled from school, further mistakes saw him serve time in prisons in the US and the UK. But from this inauspicious start, and with the help of support from The Prince's Trust, he launched successful accountancy software business KashFlow within four years of being released. Five years later, his business had signed up 10,000 customers and Jackson was named a 2011 Young Gun.

Although young women do seem somewhat under-represented among the start-up success stories, inspirational entrepreneurs such as founder of Nails Inc Thea Green (2003 Young Gun), Skimlinks' Alicia Navarro (2010) and Sweaty Betty's Tamara Hill-Norton (2005) serve as role models and encouragement for young entrepreneurial women, and last year's Young Guns - including Jude Ower of PlayMob, Julia Fowler of EDITD and Clare Johnston of Up Group - provide hope that the gender disparity will begin to lessen.

And although there is no typical entrepreneur, and there is no typical successful business, this isn't to say that the stories in the previous chapters aren't crammed full of lessons and inspiration for entrepreneurs, or aspiring entrepreneurs, young or old.

Starting a business

Starting a business can be a daunting prospect: the idea may be there but the very first steps can be difficult to take – how does one register a company? Find a domain name? Start researching the market? Or even hire the first employee? Luckily, compared with even 20 years ago, anyone wanting to start a business is much more able to access the information they need. The internet, of course, has removed the mystery from these processes: resources such as Startups.co.uk and Smarta.com can be invaluable. But help can be found from a myriad of different sources. Ross Williams, founder of Global Personals, says: 'I find it unbelievable that people don't soak up all the stuff readily available,' advising aspiring entrepreneurs to devour 'podcasts and audio books, business books, *Dragons' Den* . . .'

Rigorously test your business idea.

Of course, all the information in the world won't help a wannabe Branson if their idea isn't sufficiently thought through. Co-founder of Notonthehighstreet.com Sophie Cornish says her number one tip to young people looking to start out in business is to 'rigorously test your business idea. Ask people you trust, and people you don't know too, to give you honest feedback. Adapt and develop your business until it becomes something that really feels like it's going to work.' 2003 Young Gun Richard Reed's way of doing this (along with the other Innocent co-founders) was to give free smoothies to strangers, asking them to decide whether or not their product was good enough to base a business on. In that case, famously, the wisdom of crowds proved spot-on.

Not all, or in fact many, of the entrepreneurs in the preceding pages had a plentiful supply of spare cash with which to launch their businesses. Accessing start-up capital can take some ingenuity, or at least a willingness to take on personal debt. Ross Williams and his business partner, for example, put start-up costs on personal credit cards, juggling the debt between them until the first money started to trickle in. The traditional 'friends and family' round proved important for firms such as Ten Group - which is now speeding towards a goal of £100m turnover within three to five years. Azhar Saddique, Young Gun of 2009 and founder of UK Equipment Direct, began trading from his bedroom after accepting a £2,500 redundancy package. James Keay made ends meet when founding Select-a-skip by working evening shifts in Little Chef for £3 an hour. When he was a Young Gun in 2003, his company was turning over around £10m a year. And selling his flat to finance Fruit for the Office might have been a risky move, but it paid off for 2010 Young Gun Daniel Ox.

The stories in this book also remind us that bringing a business to life is a rocky road. There will almost inevitably be times when the bleak outlook will sometimes appear overwhelming, and the prospect of failure looms large. In these times, Ten Group founder Andrew Long has this advice: 'Don't give up. I'm lucky in that I spend a lot of time with entrepreneurs and the ones that make it are those who dogmatically won't take no for an answer and have a very clear vision.' He adds that: 'We have always had a very clear vision of what we want to do and how we want to do it.' The extent to which Long has lived by this strategy becomes apparent when it's taken into consideration that his business actually closed down in 2003, after a promised large contract failed to materialise. He and business partner Alex Cheatle scraped together enough funds to start all over again, and haven't looked back since.

Growing a business

It isn't easy to start a business. But it's arguably even harder to turn a start-up into a sustainable, scalable firm dealing with the challenges - both exciting and mundane - of fast growth and expansion. Young people often go into business to bring a fantastic idea to life. They thrive off the buzz of living on the edge between runaway success and crashing and burning. They can pitch with all the enthusiasm and passion in the world. They work tirelessly to create their product, and eulogise to great effect to press, investors and potential customers. But entrepreneurs have to be honest with themselves about their ability and willingness to stay the course once their business has gained some traction and the initial start-up buzz dissipates. The fact that so many entrepreneurs in this book have made this transition shows that young people can make excellent CEOs of established companies - but how?

As with starting a business, growing one requires advice – and lots of it. Some fortunate entrepreneurs have been able to call on the expertise of industry veterans who have joined the board as investors. Brent Hoberman, co-founder of Lastminute.com, joined the board of WAYN, for example, after investing in the business founded by 2007 Young Gun Jerome Touze and partner Peter Ward.

Such advice is particularly critical for young people, who are more likely to lack in-depth business experience. Suranga Chandratillake, founder of Blinkx, explains: 'There are two aspects of being a good CEO: domain knowledge and experience. I had a lot of domain knowledge [but] I had no management experience, or any experience in raising capital.'

His way of dealing with this was to find others with the experience he lacked. 'I supplemented that with the right mentors,' he says. 'The board really helped me, people who weren't involved in the company day to day. You need to surround yourself with the right advisers, not necessarily someone in the company – because they are too caught up in it – but someone who cares about you and who isn't too blinkered by what's going on.'

Blinkx is one of a number of Young Guns' businesses that were one of the very first players in their market: Monitise, Maximuscle and Notonthehighstreet.com also led the pack from the start. Blinkx's single-minded focus on innovating has certainly been a hugely significant factor in its continued rise. 'In our industry you simply can't stand still,' says Chandratillake. 'No matter how successful you are today, you have to be thinking of tomorrow and the next day. Even companies as large and as profitable as Google have to do the same.'

No matter how successful you are today, you have to be thinking of tomorrow and the next day.

Complacency is surely the enemy of start-up success – and the journeys of so many Young Guns pay testament to the importance of a continual striving for the new and the improved. Innovative is a word that many associate with cutting-edge digital and tech start-ups, but it is important for all businesses: from retailers to accountancy firms. Jamie Waller credits much of the success of his bailiff firm JBW, which has displayed year-on-year growth of around 20% and has achieved a turnover of £16m, to its constant innovation. 'We have been the only company in our sector to deliver new products and services consistently since formation,' he says, proving that a company doesn't need to be a Silicon Roundabout tech start-up to be an innovator. 'We invest in research and development all of the time and have people dedicated to this.'

Frequently, innovation can manifest itself in the simplest of ways. World First, for example, the business of 2007 Young Gun Nick Robinson, has carved a niche for itself among legions of foreign exchange companies simply by being committed to making the customer experience as pleasant as possible – a priority the sector is not known for. Thea Green has kept her Nails Inc products on-trend and original by creating new nail varnish effects: her customers' nails can show off a leather look, 3D effects or nail jewellery, for example. Even sectors as traditional as confectionery can be shaken up with something completely new: 2012 Young Gun Dan Shrimpton and co-founder Mike Stevens created a range of mints, gum and sweets that are different because they are made from natural ingredients and are the healthiest option on the market. Simply put, whether they innovate with their product offering, or in the way they operate, successful businesses set themselves apart from the competition.

To be running an established business displaying impressively fast growth is many entrepreneurs' dream. But it's a risky business. 'Too much, too soon' has been the downfall of many a small firm, with the danger of losing track of the bottom line ever present. Expenses can quickly spiral out of control – whether they are due to aggressive hiring, expansion into new markets, diversification into new product lines or new services, acquisitions or countless other drains on capital. Equally, expanding before a business's model has been rigorously tested, or into markets of which the management hasn't sufficient knowledge, or diversifying into an area the business does not excel in, can also spell disaster.

Our real growth through the financial crisis is international.

Again, here the Young Guns can provide advice and inspiration, with sustainable, stable growth having been displayed by many of their businesses. Many firms in the preceding chapters show how to accept large injections of external capital and ensure that the business doesn't get blown off course. Others demonstrate that growing organically, through revenues, can still be a path to impressive growth rates. One such is James Gorfin, co-founder of recruitment firm G2, who says his business could feasibly open new offices in multiple different territories around the world.

But the company will only open a new office when there's a member of staff who has worked his or her way up through the ranks and has proved capable of taking on the responsibility of managing their own office. Ten Group, founded by 2009 Young Gun Andrew Long, has expanded internationally, but will only enter a new territory once it has won a contract there, thereby minimising the risks posed by the expensive launch process. Many other firms in the preceding chapters, though no longer particularly new, have started expanding into new territories only recently – ensuring that their UK operation is running as smoothly as possible in order to be able to replicate that success elsewhere.

But international expansion, in whatever form, has been of crucial importance to the continued growth of many businesses in recent years. The economic environment has meant that many have struggled to grow in the UK or Europe – for small firms around the country, even retaining the same level of custom has been a struggle and an achievement in itself. So those who have looked at brighter markets have been rewarded. Ten Group is reaping the rewards of focusing on Asia, with Young Gun Andrew Long now working as CEO in the Asia-Pacific market. He says the region is where they see the big growth opportunities today: '[In the UK] we've managed to retain all our top clients . . . but we haven't seen new contracts going out to tender . . . But our real growth through the financial crisis is international. There's been no market in Europe.' 2003 Young Gun Thea Green is among those also looking towards the region, having spied opportunities to grow her phenomenally successful Nails Inc.

However, the US market will always hold an allure for UK entrepreneurs. Its sheer size makes it impossible to ignore. Young Guns who have expanded Stateside include Global Personal's Ross Williams, Monitise's Alastair Lukies, and World First's Nick Robinson. Tony Rafferty, founder of Printing.com, plans to open for business there soon, as does Blinkx's Suranga Chandritillake. In most cases, the US holds game-changing potential for small firms, so the importance of being sufficiently prepared is paramount.

It is a truism that, when asked for the secrets of their rise to the top, many business owners answer with one word: people. Building up the right team is an area in which an investment of time and money is likely to be amply repaid. Many Young Guns have named seeing their staff – particularly the early hires – rise to the top, to take positions of responsibility and management, as something in which they take particular pride. Cultivating and maintaining a distinct culture is difficult, particularly as a business grows. But companies such as Innocent, which – along with giants such as

Google – has raised the bar when it comes to workplace environment, are able to take their pick of the talented and enthusiastic. Happy employees reap dividends. And, as proof of that, the Young Gun companies that were named in the 2012 *Sunday Times* 100 Best Small Companies to Work For include Market Makers, Mind Candy, TBG Digital, Forward Internet Group, the Fresh Group and Steak Media. It may seem counterintuitive that it is the businesses started by younger people that perform so well when it comes to employee satisfaction, but, as the Fresh Group co-founder and 2003 Young Gun Charlie Osmond demonstrates, it could be another bonus of youthful idealism: 'We have always tried to create somewhere we're proud of and from where people get a lot of satisfaction and great careers . . . we were two idealistic 21-year-olds to whom that was important.'

Some of the profiles in the previous pages tell stories that ended with the business closing its doors. But even among the most successful, there are plenty of examples of things not going to plan. In many cases, something that appeared to spell disaster for a business ended up being something the founders could manage – and even come out of in a stronger position. When Zef Eisenberg's Maximuscle was the subject of negative press attention after being wrongfully implicated in athletes' positive drug tests, he fought back, armed with more verifications, facts and figures than could possibly be doubted. As a result, he turned the situation into invaluable positive PR for his products. Innocent's branding has been a key driver of its incredible success and was strong enough to see the company ride through the negative attention it received when it sold a majority stake to Coca-Cola. Simply having the guts and the temerity to hang on in there when others are prophesising doom and gloom can be one of the most important attributes an entrepreneur can cultivate.

Another quality almost invariably displayed by the most successful business owners is, of course, hard graft. The Young Guns in this book have poured their heart and soul into their businesses. And what is a successful business? Many of the most successful entrepreneurs in this book set the bar pretty high. Andrew Long puts it simply: 'You have to be willing to invest your whole life in it. To work 50 or 60 hours a week and to be on call seven days a week. You can grow a business without it, but it's unlikely ever to be world-changing.'

Appendix One: The Young Guns, year by year

All the Young Guns award-winners.
Name of winner, (age at the time of winning), name of company.

2003

Toby Ash (34), New Heights
Emily Bliss (35), The Brave Film Company
Richard Cobbold (34), Digital View
Lynn Cosgrave (33), TrusttheDJ
Damian Cox (28), EK Straas
Jack Glendinning (32), Its Tiles
Thea Green (27), Nails Inc
Yasmin Halai (31), Ideal Solutions Systems
Stephen Hall (34), Gamestation
Nina Hampson (30), Myla
Ben Hardyment (32), webflix.co.uk
Shelim Hussain (30), Eurofoods
Martin Jones (31), Freedom Direct
James Keay (31), Select-a-skip
Nasa Khan (30), The Accessory People
David Kilpatrick (34), Edenbrook
Scott Lloyd (28), Next Generation Group
Peter Marson (32), 4C Associates
Mark Mills (33), Cardpoint
Daniel Mitchell (33), The Source
Charlie Osmond (26), FreshMinds
Mayank Patel (35), Currencies Direct
Robin Powell (34), Moslon Holdings
Tony Rafferty (35), Printing.com
Richard Reed (30), Innocent Drinks

Serena Rees (34), Agent Provocateur
Michael Ross (34), figleaves.com
Nick Rutter (31), Sprue Aegis
Chirag Shah (32), Trading Partners
Michael Acton Smith (28), Mind Candy

2004

Matthew Bayfield (30), Tree
Seb Bishop (30), Espotting Media
Graham Bucknall (33), Adventi
Jason Butler (33), Jump
Tony Caldeira (34), Caldeira
Preet Chahal (35), ihotdesk
John Chasey (33), Iomo
Daniel Drury (33), WebAbacus
Paul Ephremsen (34), Ideal Promotions
Darren Epstein (33), Cards Inc
Simon Franks (33), Redbus
Richard Freedman (32), ACS Clothing
Chris Fung (31), Crussh
Stacey-Lea Golding (30), Premier Cru
Al Gosling (33), Extreme Group
Paul Hawkins (30), Hawk-Eye Innovations
Liz Jackson (31), Great Guns Marketing
Dr Aydin Kurt-Elli (30), Lumison
Shaid Luqman (35), Pearl Holdings (Europe)
Angus MacKinnon (30), Nowwashyourhands
Imraan Malik (28), iBetX
Nick McCulloch (28), Nickknows.com
Gary McWilliam (34), The Hire Supply Company
James Murray (34), Alternative Networks
Sophie Oliver (31), Coco Ribbon
Claire Page (34), Whitewater
Jef Richards (30), Galleria RTS
Dan Somers (30), VC-Net
Richard Stubbs (34), UK Explorer
David Williams (35), Avanti Screenmedia

2005

Patrice Barbedette (33), Jobpartners
Emma Barnett (31), Essential Escapes
Ed Bartlett (29), IGA Worldwide
Damian Bentley (32), Snowball
Tim Clyde (32), The Minimart
Wesley Cornell (23), Shopcall
Simon Coyle (30), Kshocolat
Tom Dawes (29), Aerogistics Group
James Day (24), Urban Golf
Ravi Gehlot (22), OneOffice
Heidi Gosman (33), Heidi Klein
Justin Hamilton-Martin (33), 8el
Ella Heeks (27), Abel & Cole
James Hibbert (35), Dress2kill
Tamara Hill-Norton (34), Sweaty Betty
Jennifer Irvine (29), Pure Package
Keith Jordan (31), Adwalker
Sheldon Kaye (35), Eurosimm
Timothy Maltin (32), Hardy Amies
Sarah McVittie (27), RE5ULT
Andrew Michael (24), Fasthosts
Alex Michelin (29), Finchatton
Nick Mordin (25), 24-7 Parking
James Murray Wells (22), Glasses Direct
John O'Malia (35), Trident Gaming
Mark Onyett (33), TDX Group
Andrew Pearce (32), Powwownow
Chris Philp (29), Clearstone
Sharon Richey (32), LoewyBe
Nick Wood (27), Fruitboost

2006

Hasfa Abubacker (32), Pitch TV
William Berry (30), AccomodationForStudents.com
Oliver Bishop (29), Steak Media
Jeremy Bygrave (32), Mediaburst

Jo Chalker (35), X Bar
Suranga Chandratillake (28), Blinkx TV
Anthony Cook (28), Mobile Fun
Pepita Diamand (34), Wrapit
Christina Domecq (29), SpinVox
Ben Drury (30), 7digital
Zef Eisenberg (33), Maximuscle
Jonathan Evans (25), Martinez & Partners
Sean Fergusson (34), Brandedmedia
Nick Garlick (32), Nebulas Security
Ben Grant (26), Addirect
Rob Hamilton (32), Instant Offices Group
Terry Hogan (35), New-Car-Discount.com
Barry Houlihan (34), Mobile Interactive Group
Martin Hunt (16), Hunt For It
Harjeet Johal (26), Underfivepounds.com
Jennie Johnson (34), Kids Allowed
Paul King (35), G2 Recruitment
James Layfield (32), The Lounge
Russell Lux (29), Luxtech
Simon Mansell (27), TBG Digital
Cary Marsh (34), Mydeo
David Springall (32), YoSpace
Helen Stokes (34), Morgan Hunt
Simon Tate (29), Kew Health and Beauty
Russell Taylor (29), Grafton House

2007

Ben Allan (31), The Insert & Leaflet Team (TILT)
Tom Allason (26), eCourier
Alexander Amosu (32), Amosu Luxury Phones, Mobscasino.tv, Mind of an Entrepreneur
Steve Andrews (29), SimpliGroup
Gemma Bertenshaw (29), Qdos Developments
Nick Claxson (30), Comtec Enterprises
Laurence Collins (35), activ8 intelligence
Andrew Crawford (35), The Book Depository
Scott Davies (33), Million-2-1

Amy Farren (27), MOMA Foods
Jo Groves (29), Active Digital
Nichola Lawton (28), DNA Clinics
Robert Leggett (35), Omni Resource Management Solutions
Claire Lewis (23), Truffle Shuffle
Alastair Lukies (33), Monitise
Matt McNeill (26), Sign-up.to, eTickets.to
Raj Rana (30), Itihaas
Matthew Riley (33), Daisy Communications
Nick Robinson (33), World First
Tom Savage (27), Bright Green Talent, Blue Ventures, Make Your Mark With A Tenner, Tiptheplanet.com
Rob Small (31), Miniclip
Dominic Speakman (31), Destinology
Matthew Stevenson (31), Reef One
Jerome Touze (27), Where Are You Now (WAYN)
Haani Ul Hasnain (29), Haani Cables
Shaa Wasmund (35), Brightstation Ventures, Osoyou, Miomi
Ben Way (27), The Rainmakers, Brightstation Ventures, ViaPost, The Horsesmouth
Michael Welch (28), Black Circles
Stewart Yates (35), TFM Networks
Elliott Zissman (32), Totally Fitness

2008

Stephen Abel (33), Parcels4Delivery, Parcel Shipping Manager
Oli Barrett (30), Various
Nick Bell (24), Quick.tv
Jonathon Burrows (26), Ask4
Tim Campbell (31), The Bright Ideas Trust
Kate Craig-Wood (31), Memset
Sarah Curran (35), my-wardrobe.com
William Davies (34) and Nick Bizley (33), Aspect Maintenance
Gavin Dein (32), Reward
Tim Drake (35), Flipside Group
Balthazar Fabricius (29), Fitzdares
Adam Goodyer (30) and James Perkins (30), Concert Live
Adam Hildreth (23), Crisp Thinking

Neil Hutchinson (30), TrafficBroker, Forward
Satish Jayakumar (29) and Michael Stephanblome (35), AdJug
Robert Leigh (29), Devono Property
Rupert Loman (25), Eurogamer
Dan McGuire (27), Broadbean Technology
Vincent McKevitt (29), Tossed
Fiona McLean (32) and Clare Thommen (29), Boudiche
Richard Moross (30), Moo
Lyndon Nicholson (35) and Dale Smith (31), Article 10
Ryan Notz (33), MyBuilder
Alistair Powell (26), 7CI (Seven Continent Investment)
Sumon Sadhu (25), Snaptalent
Kulbir Sohi (35) and Purvinder Tesse (35), FCL UK
Mitesh Soma (32), Chemist Direct
Holly Tucker (31), Notonthehighstreet.com
Tim Wallis (35) and Craig Beard (35), Content and Code
Max Williams (25) and Damien Tanner (21), New Bamboo

2009

Christian Arno (30), Lingo24
Warren Bennett (28) and David Hathiramani (28), A Suit That Fits
Graham Bosher (27), Graze
Alexandra Burns (35), For Your Eyes Only Portraits
Nirmal Chhabria (27), Niva International
Ali Clabburn (34), liftshare
Fraser Doherty (20), SuperJam
Simon Duffy (32) and Rhodri Ferrier (30), Bulldog Natural Grooming
Scott Fletcher (35), ANS Group
Matt Hagger (30), e-Man, Bizk.it, Zkatter
Imran Hakim (31), iTeddy
Angus Hewlett (32), FXpansion Audio UK
Priya Lakhani (28), Masala Masala
Peter Leiman (30) and Cameron Ogden (31), Blink
Andrew Long (33), Ten Lifestyle Management
Azhar Majid Saddique (31), UK Equipment Direct
Tom Marchant, James Merrett and Matt Smith (all 30), Black Tomato
Andy McLoughlin (30) and Alastair Mitchell (32), Huddle
Jimmy Metta (29), Vanquish Wine

Crispin Moger (34), Young Marmalade
Oli Norman (31), DADA
Kieran O'Neill (21), Playfire
Jack Ostrowski (33), Yellow Octopus
Sokratis Papafloratos (30), TrustedPlaces
Will Saville (33) and Richard Paterson (33), BrightStarr
Susanna Simpson (31), Limelight Public Relations
James Taylor (27), SportStars
Matt Waller (34), Benefex
James Watt (26) and Martin Dickie (26), BrewDog

2010

Sam Barnett (27), Struq
Damon Bonser (32), Spinning Hat
Antony Chesworth (30), EKM Systems
Sam Conniff (32), Livity
Matt Connolly (33), Enable Interactive
Julie Diem Le (33), Zoobug
Wesley Downham (32) and Peter Harrison (27), FGH Security
Stephen Fitzpatrick (32), Ovo Energy
Hayley Gait-Golding (30), BEAR
Justin Gayner (34), Wil Harris (28) and Barney Worfolk-Smith (35), ChannelFlip
Andy Gilbert (29), Node 4
Neal Harrison (35), Convergence Group
Karen Hastings (35), Cupcake
Dan Houghton (33) and Eric Partaker (35), Chilango
Adam King (33) and Jake Allen (31), King & Allen
Anthony Lau (29), Cyclehoop
Ning Li (30), Chloè Macintosh (37) and Julien Callède (29), Made.com
Daniel Lowe (31), UKSolutions
Claire Mason (35), Man Bites Dog
Tim Morgan (34), Picklive
Alicia Navarro (35), Skimlinks
Daniel Ox (30), Fruit for the Office
Mitesh Patel (32), Fifosys
Michael Phillips (34), ConsumerChoices.co.uk
Neil Tierney (32), Onzo

Jason Trost (29), Smarkets
Jamie Waller (31), JBW Group
Nicko Williamson (29), Climatecars
Sezer Yurtseven (30), Pan Energy Markets

2011

Christopher Baker-Brian (24) and Mansoor Mohammad Hamayun (22), BBOXX
Emily Bendell (30), BlueBella
Simon Best (32), BaseKit
Rob Booth (35), In Call Solutions
Jonathan Bramley (35), In Your Space
James Connelly (25), Fetch Media
Warren Cowan (34), Greenlight
Rob Durkin (25), FusePump
Henry Erskine Crum (28) and Alexander Will (28), Spoonfed Media
Anthony Eskinazi (28), Park At My House
David Excell (30), Featurespace
Kevin Flood (22) and Mike Harty (23), Shopow
Emi Gal (25), Brainient
David Grimes (28) and Paul Haydock (28), myParcelDelivery.com
Ian Hogarth, Pete Smith and Michelle You (all 29), Songkick
Duane Jackson (32), KashFlow
Damian Kimmelman (29), Duedil
David Langer (26) and Andy Young (26), GroupSpaces
Steve Lowy (30), Umi Hotels
Joshua March (25), Conversocial
Tom Morgan (34), MVF Global
Mark Pearson (31), MyVoucherCodes
James Robinson (30), Zeffa
Emma Sinclair (29), Target Parking
Lucian Tarnowski (27), BraveNewTalent
Paul Thomas (29) and Henry Braithwaite (29), Market Makers
Charlie Walker (27), Vivid Resourcing
Heather Wilkinson (32), Striding Out
Ross Williams (33), Global Personals
Jamie Woods (28), JCW

2012

Rajesh Agrawal (34), RationalFX
Richard Baister (30), SUMO Drinks
Lee Biggins (34) and Brian Wakem (32), CV Library
Jay Bregman (33), Hailo
Callum Bush (26), MediaDevil
Alistair Crane (26), Grapple Mobile
Samir Desai, James Meekings and Andrew Mullinger (all 29), Funding Circle
Ben Donnelly (34), Elixir Group
George Graham (26) and Henry Graham (31), Wolf & Badger
Vinay Gupta (31) and Tom Wright (33), WhipCar
Chris Harrison (33), Collstream
Taavet Hinrikus (30) and Kristo Käärmann (31), Exchange Solutions, Transferwise
Dr Shamus Husheer (35) and Dr Oriane Chausiaux (31), Cambridge Temperature Concepts (trading as DuoFertility)
Clare Johnston (31), Up Group
Adrian Kinnersley (34), Twenty Recruitment
Felix Leuschner (30), Stylistpick
Greg Marsh (33) and Tim Davey (35), onefinestay
Dr Ben Medlock (32) and Jon Reynolds (26), SwiftKey (trading as Touch Type)
Matt Miller (34), ustwo
Tom O'Hagan (35), Virtual1
Will Orr-Ewing (27), Keystone Tutors
Jude Ower (31), PlayMob
Dan Shrimpton (34), Peppersmith
Lyndsey Simpson (34), The Curve Group
James Street (27) and Neil Waller (28), My Destination
Chris Tanner (32) and Andrew Mulvenna (33), Brightpearl
Tom Valentine (31), Secret Escapes
Erich Wasserman (35), MediaMath
Geoff Watts (35) and Julia Fowler (31), EDITD (Stylescape)
Ben Whitaker, Tom Godber and Ed Howson (all 34), Masabi

Appendix Two: The companies behind the Young Guns awards

Farrer & Co.

Farrer & Co.'s Entrepreneurs and Family Business Group provides specialist legal advice on the full range of issues entrepreneurs might face, spanning private client, corporate, family, financial services, disputes, IP and residential and commercial property.

We are one of only a few law firms able to offer genuinely market-leading expertise in all of these areas - all under one roof and readily available to collaborate to achieve a rapid solution.

We can advise on setting up, developing and growing businesses, as well as bringing in external funding and maintaining control for the next generation, all done in the most tax-efficient way possible. We have very strong relationships with our entrepreneurial clients, relationships that have been built up over time thanks to our consistently strong track record and in-depth market knowledge.

For more information, please contact Richard Lane on 020 3375 7548 or at richard.lane@farrer.co.uk.

haysmacintyre

haysmacintyre is a successful firm of chartered accountants and tax advisers based in central London, providing quality accountancy, tax, corporate finance and business advice to entrepreneurs and fast growing businesses. The 25 partners lead a team of 160 staff advising start-ups, fast growing and entrepreneurial businesses, international groups, listed companies and social enterprises on a range of commercial and financial challenges.

With over a third of our partners under 40, we are a youthful firm with a reputation for being dynamic and forward-thinking. Our professionals work in specific sectors that include creative, media and technology, hospitality, real estate, financial services and social enterprises, so clients benefit from advisers familiar with their industries and already connected to other key professional advisers. Our long-standing involvement with Young Guns, coupled with our own experience of working with entrepreneurs and business owners, means that we have a thorough understanding of issues facing growing businesses so we can support them at every stage from starting up, through growth and diversification, to floating on the stock market or another event. As a founding firm of a large international alliance of accountants and lawyers, we source reliable, local expertise wherever in the world our clients are growing their businesses and we assist international companies doing business in the UK.

haysmacintyre has sponsored Young Guns since 2007 and is closely involved in the project from nomination stage, through finalist selection, and then to celebrating the announcement of the haysmacintyre 'Top Gun'.

Visit www.haysmacintyre.com to find out more.

Keystone Law

Established in 2002, Keystone Law is a full-service law firm with over 120 senior solicitors. We help entrepreneurs and growing businesses across most business sectors.

Keystone is also a firm with a genuine difference, an award-winning business model and a level of service that is second to none. Our clever use of technology, in particular, drives efficiencies while reducing overheads, administration and duplication.

Our hands-on service and innate flexibility make us the ideal choice for developing businesses with challenges that are often many and varied. We routinely support such entities from start-up, through the growth phase and to sale or merger. If there are problems along the way, then our dispute resolution team has the expertise to help.

Keystone solicitors have all previously worked at the country's top law firms for at least 10 years. Our clients appreciate the experience of senior lawyers who have come across similar issues before and they never feel that they are paying for someone to learn on the job.

We are a truly modern business that leverages technology to provide a level of service and value that is hard to find nowadays. As a result, we continue to be one of the country's fastest growing law firms.

Keystone is delighted to be sponsoring Young Guns 2013 for the first of what will hopefully be many occasions.